Thomas Cook

Travellers

MALLORCA

BY
NIGEL TISDALL

Produced by
Thomas Cook Publishing

Written by Nigel Tisdall
Updated by Lura Seavey
Original photography by Peter Baker
Original design by Laburnum Technologies Pvt Ltd

Editing and page layout by Cambridge Publishing
Management Ltd, Unit 2, Burr Elm Court,
Caldecote CB3 7NU
Series Editor: Karen Beaulah

Published by Thomas Cook Publishing
A division of Thomas Cook Tour Operations Ltd

PO Box 227, The Thomas Cook Business Park,
Units 15–16, Coningsby Road,
Peterborough PE3 8SB, United Kingdom
E-mail: books@thomascook.com
www.thomascookpublishing.com
Tel: +44 (0) 1733 416477

ISBN-13: 978-1-84157-442-4
ISBN-10: 1-84157-442-2

Text © 2006 Thomas Cook Publishing
Maps © 2006 Thomas Cook Publishing
First edition © 2003 Thomas Cook Publishing
Second edition © 2006 Thomas Cook Publishing

Head of Thomas Cook Publishing: Chris Young
Project Editor: Linda Bass
Production/DTP Editor: Steven Collins

Printed and bound in Spain by: Grafo Industrias Gráficas, Basauri.

Cover design by: Liz Lyons Design, Oxford.
Front cover credits: Left © Westend61/Alamy; centre © Balearic images/Alamy;
right © FAN&MROSS Travelstock/Alamy
Back cover credits: Left © Getty Images; right © Thomas Cook Tour Operations Ltd

Contents

KEY TO MAPS	
✈	Airport
☀	Viewpoint (*mirador*)
⌐⌐	City walls
★	Start of walk/tour
[i]	Information
C713	Road number
203m ▲	Mountain

Introduction

Mallorca might have been invented by a team of tourism gurus locked in a *tapas* bar with a brief to come up with a holiday island that would please as many people as possible.

As a well-established Mediterranean resort it has everything you would expect: good sandy beaches, guaranteed summer sunshine, safe water for swimming and accommodation to suit all pockets. If you like pretty mountain villages and photogenic harbours, watersports, golf courses and excursions in glass-bottomed boats and intimate fish restaurants – they are all here.

But there is more, a Mallorca that scarcely needs the cooing of the brochures. Palma, the capital, has a dramatic seafront cathedral and old streets with a whiff of history. There are enthralling underground caves and isolated hilltop monasteries to seek out, epic mountains much-loved by walkers and cyclists, and marshes and offshore islands that regularly draw birdwatchers.

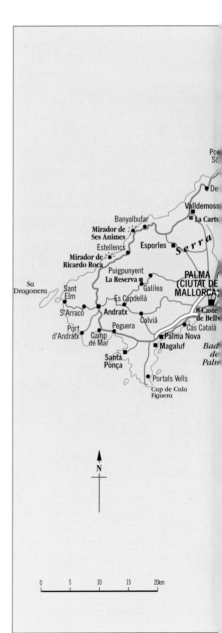

Away from the coastal resorts, life in villages is blissfully tranquil

industry and factories manufacturing shoes, garments and costume jewellery provide employment, but tourism is the overwhelming mainstay of the island's economy.

Wildlife

The star character of Mallorcan wildlife has long been extinct. Six million years ago, Myotragus stalked the Balearic Islands, a peculiarly-shaped antelope with eyes at the front of its head and buck teeth that functioned like a pickaxe. In comparison, the creatures currently scurrying around Mallorca appear unexciting: four types of snake (all non-poisonous), a rarely seen spotted civet cat, goats, hares and rabbits, frogs, toads and various insects. Only on the island of Cabrera, a protected wilderness, do a few endemic species of lizard arouse the visitor's curiosity.

Look skyward though, and it's a different picture. Mallorca is of great interest to ornithologists and birdwatchers, and flocks of binocular-addicts regularly descend on the island in April and May during the migration season. Hoopoes, Eleonora's falcons, black vultures, red kites and several types of eagle cause particular excitement. Diverse habitats that include wetlands, saltpans, rocky cliffs and offshore islets, as well as the woods and forests of Mallorca's mountains, enhance the appeal of the island to both birds and their admirers.

Hunting remains popular with a powerful section of the community: wild goats, rabbits, quail, turtle doves, wood pigeon, partridges, mallards and

The hoopoe: frequently seen in Mallorca

coots are some of the targets. The wholesale slaughter of migrating thrushes, using purpose-made nets known as *filats de coll,* is also permitted. Farmers consider the olive-loving birds a pest, while cooks see them as a country delicacy. Restrictions were recently introduced to promote more responsible hunting – a heavy fine has been imposed on the killing of black vultures, which were once in danger of extinction here.

As in so many parts of the Mediterranean, wildlife and the natural landscape are under threat from development. Fortunately, through the efforts of the environmental group GOB (Grupo Ornithologia Balear) and the local authorities, almost a third of the island is now under protection.

Talayot Culture

The Balearic Islands were originally settled by an industrious and well-organised people – who left enigmatic visiting cards around Mallorca known as *talayots*. These megalithic monuments get their name from *atalaya*, the Arab word for a watchtower, and have become eponymous symbols of the talented civilisation that flourished here during the Bronze Age.

The Talayot Period came in three waves. Pre-Talayot culture started around 2000 BC and was principally cave-based. By 1500 BC *navetes* (burial chambers that resemble upturned boats) were being constructed: there are abundant examples on Menorca. The most creative phase, the Talaiotic, lasted from 1300 BC until about 800 BC and coincided with the emergence of a more violent and hierarchical society. A third stage, Late Talayot, is characterised by the construction of *taulas*, colossal table-like stone structures which are well

preserved on Menorca. By the 6th century BC, Talayot culture was on the wane as the islands came under the influence of the Greeks and Phoenicians.

Archaeological research and evidence from similar cultures in Sardinia and Corsica suggest that life in Talayot times was surprisingly sophisticated. The islanders kept sheep, pigs and cattle, constructed ingenious wells, and made a delicate, decorated pottery.

Talayots were built to both circular and quadrangular plans, and were most likely constructed as main residences and observation posts in the islands' fortified settlements. On Mallorca, the best opportunities to inspect them are at Capocorb Vell and Ses Païsses.

Archaeological finds from the period, including ceramics, weapons, tools and jewellery, can be seen in the Museu de Mallorca in Palma and the Museu Regional in Artà.

There is order in the seeming disorder of the Talayot ruins at Capocorb Vell

History

5000 BC	Remains found in caves near Sóller and Valldemossa indicate the presence of humans on the island.
1300–800 BC	Talayot culture flourishes in Mallorca and Menorca, leaving behind enigmatic stone towers and ruined dwellings at sites such as Capocorb Vell and Ses Païsses.
1000–123 BC	Phoenician, Greek and Carthaginian traders visit the Balearics: the name probably derives from the Greek verb *ballein*, meaning 'to throw' – a reference to the leather slings used as deadly weapons by the islanders.
123 BC–AD 425	Roman commander Quintus Cecilius Metullus conquers Mallorca. The island is called Balearis Major (hence its modern name) with the capital in Pollentia, now Alcúdia, site of a surviving Roman theatre. Christianity takes hold during the 2nd century AD.
425–707	With the decline of the Roman Empire, Mallorca comes under Vandal and Byzantine rule.
707–1229	Raids by the Moors accompany their conquest of mainland Iberia – by 902 Mallorca is part of the Emirate of Córdoba. The Moors build mosques, palaces and gardens and introduce sophisticated agricultural methods using windmills and waterwheels. In Palma, then known as Medina Mayurqa, the Banys Àrabs (Arab Baths) are a sign of their presence.

Statue of Ramón Llull

Passejada d'es Bou and **Carro Triunfal** (27th–28th): In Valldemossa, a bull is led through the streets as part of the cult of Santa Catalina Thomás. The next day, a local girl dressed as the saint takes part in a triumphal procession of carts.

August
Festa de Nostra Senyora de los Angeles (2nd): Pollença's *festa* includes a mock fight between Christians and Moors.
Festa de Sant Llorenç (10th): Selva's patron saint is honoured.
Sant Bartomeu (24th): Capdepera remembers St Bartholomew with horse racing. Devil dances in Montuïri.
Sant Agustín (28th): Dancing and horsey antics in Felanitx.
Sant Joan (29th): Sant Joan celebrates its eponymous patron with dancing and Balearic singing.
Pilgrimage on foot from Palma to Lluc.

September
Festa de Sant Mateu (21st): *Festa* in Bunyola.
Devils-versus-Saints procession in Santa Margalida (first Sunday).
Melon *festa* in Vilafranca de Bonany (second Sunday).
Binissalem's grape and wine festival; country fairs in Montuïri and Artà (last Sunday).

October
Festa d'es Botifarró (third Sunday): Botifarró sausage festival in Sant Joan.
La Beateta (16th): Costumed procession in Palma celebrating Santa Catalina Thomás. Country fairs in Alcúdia, Campos, Felanitx, Porreres and Llucmajor. Raft race in Porto Portals.

November
Dijous Bò (third Thursday): Major agricultural show in Inca.
Festa de Sant Andreu (30th): *Festa* in Santanyí.

December
Navidad (25th): Mallorcan Christmas with carol concerts and Nativity scenes.
Festa de l'Estendard (31st): Palma remembers Jaume I's capture of the city in 1229.

Ask at a tourist office for up-to-date information as dates sometimes change.

Costumed figures re-enact festive life in Mallorca

Impressions

Mallorca presents few problems to visitors, though services and facilities can get strained at peak season. To get the best out of Mallorca, spend time picking the right resort and accommodation for your needs, then use this as a base for forays to other parts of the island.

A rugged backdrop to an idyllic beach resort

When to Go
Mallorca is very much a summer holiday resort, with the season running between April and October. July and August are the peak months. If you pay a visit outside of these times be prepared for poor weather. Many of the hotels close for at least part of the winter, and the choice of excursions, restaurants and shops, and the opening hours of sights

Another hard day's sightseeing in Port de Sóller, a resort favoured by French visitors

are all considerably reduced. Great efforts are currently being made to make it attractive as a year-round destination.

However, Palma never really closes, and if lying on a sun-scorched beach is not your main objective, Mallorca can be very rewarding to visit in either spring or late autumn, when things are less hectic.

Where to Stay
Most visitors to Mallorca stay in pre-booked accommodation. Pick somewhere as close as possible to your preferred holiday option, whether the seafront in Palma, or rural isolation in a mountain farmhouse, or round-the-clock partying at resorts such as Palma Nova and S'Arenal.

Bear in mind that most resorts, though superficially international, are often favoured by one or two nationalities in particular. For example, you will find Germans mostly in S'Arenal, Scandinavians in Cala Major, the French in Port de Sóller and the British in Magaluf and Port de Pollença. Whether it is best to stay with or without your compatriots is another tough decision.

For the types of accommodation available, *see pp170–73.*

Try a tour of Palma by horse and carriage – Sunday is best, as there is less traffic

Getting Around

Wherever you stay on Mallorca, any other part of the island can be reached within a day trip. In recent years the roads have greatly improved; if you enjoy driving and like to get out into the peace of the mountains or visit the quieter beaches, it is worth hiring a car for two or three days.

While it is possible to zoom around the island in a day, the sightseeing is better taken at a leisurely pace. Four drives – covering the best of Mallorca – are included in this guide. Each one can be done in around five hours, but you should really make a day of it.

Public transport on the island is good. If you are staying outside Palma, consider taking a bus into the capital rather than paying for a car you will hardly use. Buses get to most corners of the island, and the service is generally reliable. Tourist offices can give you a free timetable. Mallorca has two railway lines, too: a historic line running from Palma through the Serra de Tramuntana to Sóller, and a half-hour run east to Inca. The line has now been extended to Sa Pobla, a 15-minute journey.

The Mallorcan Day

Organise your sightseeing around the fact that everything closes for lunch and a siesta between 1.30pm and 4.30pm. A notable exception is La Seu, Palma's cathedral, which stays open through the lunch hour in summer. Most smaller museums and art galleries close on Saturday afternoon and Sunday. In the evening, the hotter the weather, the later the locals eat. Most Mallorcans wouldn't think of eating before 9pm in summer.

The resorts live by their own laws: if there are people about and if there is money to be made, the shops and bars will stay open.

the success of tourism on the island, and the Mallorcans work hard to maintain standards in the resorts; the seafronts in Palma Nova, Magaluf and S'Arenal were recently given a facelift.

Ohe of the nicest jobs on Mallorca must be counting its beaches. The last official tally was 76, of which more than half are awarded Blue Flags by the European Union for being safe, clean and well kept. Beaches are crucial to

If you come in summer, don't waste time trying to find that undiscovered, blissfully deserted beach. It is possible to get away from (most of) it all, but you will need to park your rented car and take a long, long walk. Until recently, Platja Es Trenc in the south of the island fulfilled most people's isolationist dreams, but now even that has a car park and attendant at one end. There are no developments here, though, and it is a popular spot for nude sunbathing and swimming.

Easy to access beaches with peaceful sands at Cala Llombards (this page) and at Platja de Canyamel (facing page, above)

Nearer Palma, the tiny Platja Mago (off the road to Portals Vells) attracts a similar nudist crowd.

However, the majority of visitors are happy to join the seething, sun-wallowing masses in the resorts. The most popular beaches are those around Badia de Palma, Badia d'Alcúdia and Badia de Pollença. On the east coast the tourist centres are Cala Bona, Cala d'Or, Cala Millor and Sa Coma. *Calas* (coves) offer an enjoyable and quieter alternative to these well-known hot-spots. High, deeply-eroded cliffs often shelter the sands at the end of these small inlets. The water tends to be invitingly clear – ideal for snorkelling, diving from the rocks, and for strong swimmers who feel frustrated by the shallow waters in the larger bays. Try Cala Pi (south of Llucmajor), Cala Llombards and Cala Santanyí (both east of Santanyí), or the larger beaches at Cala Agulla and Cala Mesquida (both north of Capdepera).

FINDING THE SIGHTS

The 'What to See' section of this guide (*pp30–135*) divides Mallorca into five sections, with the sights arranged alphabetically in each. If your time is limited, you should try to spend a few hours in Palma, and make a trip by car, train or bus into the mountains of the Serra de Tramuntana. The following sights of the island are recommended.

Palma

La Seu, Palma's seafront cathedral, is the island's star sight, but find time to also visit La Llotja nearby, once the city's maritime trading exchange. A walk along the seafront and Passeig des Born, the city's traditional promenade, is the statutory introduction to the Mallorcan capital, but don't miss the Fundació La Caixa, a splendidly-restored Modernista building in Plaça Weyler.

West of Palma

Well-developed resorts run all along the coast west of Palma. Get into the mountains behind them to visit the country house of La Granja, and the tailor-made nature reserve, La

Reserva. To see Mallorca in a different light, visit Porto Portals, an elite marina for the waterborne jet-set, and the Fundació Pilar i Joan Miró, the studio of the late surrealist painter, Joan Miró.

Northwest

This is the most accessible part of the Serra de Tramuntana. Take the Palma–Sóller train and the tram ride on to Port de Sóller for an insight into island life at the start of the 20th century. The former Carthusian monastery at Valldemossa, where George Sand and Frédéric Chopin stayed during their visit of 1838–9, is an essential Mallorcan sight. The Moorish gardens at Alfabia, the spectacular descent down the northern cliffs to Sa Calobra, and the revered monastery at Lluc are all of interest.

Northeast

Try to savour the atmosphere of at least a couple of Mallorca's ancient towns, such as Alcúdia, Artà, Petra or Pollença. Here the scenic draws are the Cap de Formentor peninsula, the illuminated subterranean

Picturesque signs are common

caves at Artà and the great sandy sweep of the Badia d'Alcúdia. Nature-lovers should make for the Bóquer Valley and S'Albufera wetlands.

South

Crossing Es Pla, Mallorca's inland plain, is as crucial to understanding the island as touring its mountains. Drive up to the religious sanctuaries on Puig de Randa for an overview of this area, then relax in the quieter *calas* (coves) of the east coast. There are large caves at Drac and Hams, prehistoric ruins at Capocorb Vell, and artificial pearl and glass factories along the Palma–Manacor road. If all this sounds too much, escape on a boat to the island of Cabrera.

Sign Language

Catalan is the favoured language of the Balearic Islands, with each island claiming that its version is the oldest and purest one! Although many elderly people in the villages still do not speak Castilian Spanish, let alone write it, there is no need to learn Catalan before visiting Mallorca, but if you do make the slightest effort to learn even the smallest phrase, you will be better received.

A friendly *'Bon dia'* (good day) to passers-by in the streets or a *'Moltes gracies'* (thanks very much) in the bar or

Olive trees and a backdrop of mountains: a classic Mallorcan landscape near Andratx

Excursions

Organised coach and minibus excursions are a popular way of seeing the island. If you don't mind travelling at group pace to a pre-ordained itinerary, they are an easy way to catch the well-known sights. The choice of routes increases in the summer, when some excursions are combined with a boat trip, for instance from Port de Sóller to Sa Calobra.

Most companies offer set excursions on certain days of the week: they can be booked through your hotel, holiday representative or travel agent. Itineraries do vary, so it pays to shop around. Lunch is sometimes included in the price, but it is rarely anything to get excited about and can devour a lot of sightseeing time. Hotels can provide packed lunches, or you can simply go to a supermarket and create your own picnic.

Favourite destinations for coach tours are Valldemossa, Sa Calobra, the caves at Drac, the pearl factories at Manacor and the country house of La Granja. Trips advertised as an 'Island Tour' are rarely that comprehensive. As a rough guide, excursions venturing into the Serra de Tramuntana or out to Cap de Formentor are the most visually rewarding. It is worth remembering that you can travel under your own steam: Valldemossa is only half an hour's drive or bus ride from Palma, and to travel on the scenic Palma–Sóller train all you need to do is go to the station and buy a ticket. If you would like all the arrangements taken care of for you a good travel agency to contact is Viajes Marsans (*Passeig des Born 6, Palma. Tel: (902) 30 60 90; www.marsans.es*).

Steps lead up from the seafront to Palma's historic cathedral, La Seu, begun in 1230

shop will do wonders. And, like people all over the world, Mallorcans are only too happy to discuss the weather – a few expressive gestures in response to the warm sun beating down on you will encourage an immediate response.

Otherwise, the language creates few problems for visitors. In Palma and in the holiday resorts, most people speak English and enjoy practising it. However, if you know any Castilian Spanish, the languages remain useful. (In this book, all place-names and streets are in Catalan.)

Restful cloisters lie within the Basílica de Sant Francesç

Arab Baths are a souvenir of Medina Mayurqa, the Moorish city that once existed here from the 8th to 13th century. The baths date from the 10th century: the domed colander-like roof, originally pierced with 25 small skylights, is supported by 12 slender columns. Bathers used to move between two chambers, the hot steamy *caldarium* and the cooler *tepidarium*.
Carrer de Can Serra 3–7.
Tel: (971) 72 15 49. Follow the signs from the cathedral. Open: daily 9am–7pm. Closed: as it pleases. Admission charge.

Basílica de Sant Francesç

A statue of Junípero Serra, California's founding friar (*see pp40–41*), greets visitors to this mighty church. Behind him rises a sober, sunbaked façade, with an impressively ornate portal added in 1700. Foundations for the church and monastery of St Francis were laid in 1281, but the original ensemble was remodelled following a strike by lightning in 1580. Visitors now enter through the cloisters, reached through a building to the right (ring the bell). The cloisters are an example of the many tranquil oases that lie hidden behind the high walls of Old Palma. Lemon trees, a central well and arcades of slim Gothic pillars create a meditative ambience. In comparison, the interior of the church, with its vaulted ceiling, Baroque altar and intensely decorated side chapels, seems pompous and overblown. A focal point of interest is the spot-lit tomb of the 13th-century Mallorcan writer Ramón Llull, which is behind the altar in the first chapel on the left. His effigy rests high up in the wall, adorned by an inverted crescent symbolising his missionary work in North Africa.

Plaça Sant Francesc 6–7.
Tel: (971) 71 26 95. Open: Mon–Sat
9.30am–12.30pm & 3.30–6pm.
Sun 9.30am–noon.
Admission charge.

The mighty façade of the Basilica de Sant Francesc

Built to a rare circular design, Castell de Bellver crowns a hill to the west of Palma

Castell de Bellver (Bellver Castle)

Even today, this great castle, begun in 1309, can easily be seen from Palma's seafront. Framed by thick pinewoods, it stood as a signal to all-comers that the island's rulers were firmly in control. If you do not have a car, consider taking a taxi up, then walking back through the woods – look for the path opposite the entrance, which leads down via a chapel to Carrer de Bellver and Avinguda de Joan Miró.

Bellver means 'good view', and the opportunity to stand on its roof and survey Palma and its bay should not be missed. The castle is remarkable for its circular shape: from the air it looks like a monumental record player. Four round towers stand at the compass points, with the largest, the Tower of Homage, connected by an arch to the centre. A deep moat, which you can

walk right around, completes the defences.

The castle was used as a summer residence by the Mallorcan kings, and served for many centuries as a political prison: graffiti carved by French prisoners-of-war can still be seen on its stones. Today the atmosphere is rather sterile, but the central arcaded courtyard and sweeping stone roof above (carefully designed to feed every raindrop into a central cistern) are aesthetic marvels. Archaeological finds from round Mallorca are exhibited in some of the lower rooms. The castle is used as a popular venue for concerts in the summer, and for government receptions.
West of Avinguda Joan Miró.
Tel: (971) 73 06 57. Open: daily,
Apr–Sept 8am–9pm; Oct–Mar 8am–8pm.
Sundays & holidays limited hours vary.
Admission charge.

Window detail from La Llotja

Collecció March (March Collection)

The Mallorcan banker, Joan March, who financed Franco's uprising and became one of the world's wealthiest men, amassed a substantial modern art collection. Among the large and colourful works of Spanish contemporary art displayed here by the Fundació Joan March are works by the famous, including Picasso, Miró, Dalí and the Mallorca-born Miquel Barceló. *Carrer de Sant Miquel 11.*
Tel: (971) 71 35 15. Open: Mon–Fri 10am–6.30pm, Sat 10.30am–2pm. Closed: Sun. Free admission.

Fundació La Caixa

Palma's Gran Hotel, the city's first quality hotel, opened in 1902. Designed by the Catalan architect Lluis Domènech i Montaner, it was the first of several Modernista (Spanish Art Nouveau) buildings to grace the city. In 1993, after careful restoration by the Fundació La Caixa, it was unveiled as a stunning cultural centre staging exhibitions and musical events. Spectacularly lit up at night, it has a popular ground floor bar/café.
Plaça Weyler 3. Tel: (971) 72 01 11. Open: Tue–Sat 10am–9pm, Sun 10am–2pm. Closed: Mon. Admission charge for some events.

La Llotja (The Exchange)

Close to the seafront, La Llotja and its adjacent *plaça* (square) and garden are testimony to the maritime might that underpinned Palma's prosperity. Built between 1426 and 1456 to designs by Guillem Sagrera, who was also responsible for the cathedral's Portal del Mirador, La Llotja served as a meeting place for the shipping merchants and commercial traders who gathered in the city. A kindly guardian angel hovers over the entrance, but once you are within it is not hard to imagine a cut-throat atmosphere with insider deals being struck on the stone benches and hard-done-by merchants gazing up in despair at the palm-like pillars supporting the vaulted roof. When Palma's seafaring fortunes declined, La Llotja became a granary and is now used as a venue for cultural exhibitions.
Plaça Llotja. Palma Tourist Office. Tel: (971) 71 17 05. Open: only when there are exhibitions; check before visiting. Free admission.

this pedestrian promenade still functions as a spine dividing the city. At its southern end is Plaça de la Reina. At the north is Plaça Rei Joan Carles I, where a bizarre obelisk is supported by four minute tortoises. To the west, is the elegant Can Sollerich, a newly restored 18th-century palace. On the opposite side, Bar Bosch is a focus of city life.

Plaça del Mercat

Walk along Carrer de l'Unió to find a popular square that presents a scene typical of traditional Palma. Beneath its venerable rubber tree is a statue of Mallorca's most famous politician, Antoni Maura, a conservative prime minister of Spain several times over at the start of the 20th century. Behind him rises the belfry of the church of Sant Nicolau. To the left are two vivacious Modernista buildings, the recently restored Pensió Menorquina, and next door, the rippling Can Casasayas, now a clothes shop. Further along is the Palau de Justícia, Palma's courthouse. It was once a private palace called Can Berga. Walk into the courtyard to appreciate the capacious plan on which it was built.

Poble Espanyol (Spanish Village)

Spain in a nutshell is the objective of this architectural theme park-cum-conference facility in the west of Palma. Reproduced attractions include the Patio de los Arrayanes and Arab Baths from Granada's Alhambra, Toledo's mammoth Puerta de Bisagra and Casa de El Greco, a Canary Islands house and an *ajuntament* (town hall) from Guipúzcoa. Spain's most popular

Spanish architecture's greatest hits are paraded in the Poble Espanyol

architectural showpieces are replicated in miniature and sold as artefacts in craft workshops and souvenir shops.
Carrer de Poble Espanyol 39. Tel: (971) 73 70 75. Open: daily 9am–5.30pm. Shops closed: Sat afternoon & Sun. Admission charge. Bus: 5.

Sant Miquel

The church of Sant Miquel is one of the most popular in the city. Its plain façade dates from the 14th century. Built on the site of a mosque, it was here that Jaume I celebrated mass after capturing the city in the name of Christianity.
Carrer de Sant Miquel 2. Tel: (971) 71 54 55. Open: Mon–Sat 8am–1pm & 5–8pm, on Sun, as services permit. Free admission.

Detail from the Portal del Mirador

La Seu

Built right on the water's edge for all to see, Palma's cathedral is an expression of political power rather than religious fervour. Like the towering Palau de l'Almudaina and the mighty Castell de Bellver, La Seu was a declaration to the world that the island's Christian colonists were here to stay. It is particularly beautiful when seen from the sea, as intended, but like all great buildings it constantly surprises its onlookers. By day the sun burnishes the soft-toned sandstone of its south front; come nightfall its bony skeleton is illuminated like a rocket ship departing for the heavens.

Exterior

Work began on La Seu (the Catalan word for a bishop's see) in 1230, but it was not until 1601 that the cathedral was completed. In 1851 the west front was damaged in an earthquake. During the restoration two turrets were added, and the side rose windows and doors blocked up. The cathedral saves its best profile for the sea: a stroll along the south front provides good views of the line of pinnacled buttresses that support the central nave. The Portal del Mirador here dates from 1389 and includes a *Last Supper* in the tympanum and five statues on either side of the door by the Mallorcan sculptor, Guillem Sagrera.

Treasury

The cathedral is entered on its north side through the Portal del Almoina where alms were dispensed to the poor. This leads into the Treasury, where vast numbers of manuscripts, silverware, monstrances, processional props and holy relics are displayed. A pair of early 18th-century man-high candelabra gives a clue to the past wealth enjoyed by the Catholic church in Mallorca.

Interior

Stand with your back to the west front's rarely-opened Portal Mayor, and you will appreciate the size and rhythm of the cathedral's three naves. Supported by 14 slender octagonal pillars, the central nave soars 44m high, and the east rose window, with a diameter of 13.3m, is among the largest in the world. The glass was damaged during an air raid at the start of the Spanish Civil War. In 1902 Antoni Gaudí, architect of Barcelona's dazzling Sagrada Família church, was invited to restore the cathedral to its 14th-century glory. His reforms remain controversial: some visitors will gain spiritual uplift from the illuminated Crown of Thorns now suspended over the altar, others may feel it looks like an accident at a funfair.

Among the 14 side chapels, Nostra Senyora de la Corona (on the south side, second in from the east) has four athletic angels brought from the Carthusian monastery in Valldemossa. Other points of interest are the Plateresque stone pulpit to the north of the altar and the 110 walnut choir stalls carved in 1328. The oldest part of the cathedral, the Trinity Chapel, is behind the altar but not accessible. Inside are the tombs of Jaume II and Jaume III: times have changed since George Sand visited in 1838, when guides would open up their marble sarcophagi so that visitors could behold the mummified corpses. The exit from the cathedral leads through its neglected cloisters. Look up and you can see La Seu's 47-m high belltower. When its largest bell, which weighs over four tonnes, was rung

Gilded relief in the cathedral interior

in 1857 as a storm warning it shattered most of the cathedral's stained glass. *Carrer de Palau Reial 29. Tel: (971) 72 31 30. Open: Apr–Oct, Mon–Fri 10am–6.30pm; Nov–Mar 10am–2.30pm; Sat 10am–2pm (year round). Museum closed: Sun. Admission charge.*

The cathedral's south front once stood right at the water's edge

Walk: Historic Palma

The charm of modern Palma, once an ancient Mediterranean port city, comes from its architectural blend of Gothic, Moorish and Renaissance monuments. This introductory walk should preferably be taken in the morning when markets and churches are open. (*See map on p31 for route.*) *Allow 2 hours, excluding stops at sights and bars.*

Start at Plaça d'Espanya.

1 Plaça d'Espanya
In the centre of this transport hub of Mallorca is the equestrian statue of Jaume I, Conquistador of Mallorca. *Walk west via Plaça de la Porta Pintada to Carrer de Sant Miquel. Turn south, past the church of Santa Catalina and the Hospital Militar on the opposite corner.*

2 Mercat Olivar
Veer left into Plaça del Olivar, the city's most enjoyable market: see spectacular fish displays in the *pescaderia*. *Take Carrer de Josep Tous I Ferrer back to* Carrer de Sant Miquel, reach before 1pm.

3 Plaça Major
Look in the church of Sant Miquel (*see p45*), then follow the pedestrianised Carrer de Sant Miquel past the Collecció March (*see p38*) to the enclosed, arcaded Plaça Major, with its street entertainers and artisans' stalls. Leave by the opposite arch. Look up to the right to admire two Modernista buildings, L'Àguila and Can Forteza Rei. *Walk down Carrer de Jaume II.*

4 Plaça Cort
Carrer de Jaume II is typical of the lively

Take a breather in the cafés of Plaça Major, an arena for street performers and artisans

pedestrian shopping streets that lie east of Passeig des Born. At the bottom, turn left past the blushing edifice of Can Corbella for Plaça Cort. The square, with its wizened olive tree, is dominated by the Ajuntament (*see p34*).
Cross to take Carrer del Convent de Sant Francesç.

5 Plaça de Sant Francesç

Passing the restored 13th-century church of Santa Eulalia, you reach the Basílica de Sant Francesç (*see pp35–6*). The narrow streets here, with their high-walled, solid-door buildings, are filled with the introspective spirit of old Palma. Turn back down Carrer del Pare Nadal, then left into Carrer de Montesion to reach the Jesuit church of Montesió with its glorious and grimy Baroque façade.
Take the adjacent Carrer de Vent, turn right into Carrer de Sant Alonso and Carrer de la Puresa, then go left down Carrer de la Portella. After passing the Museu de Mallorca (see p42), note the sneering faces adorning the Hostal Isabel II as you leave the old city.

6 Parc de la Mar

Sunlight returns as you emerge by the city ramparts. Just before the arching Porta de la Portella, turn right up an incline to walk beside the south front of the cathedral, with views over the Parc de la Mar.

At the end, descend some steps and turn right into S'Hort del Rei, the shady gardens with fountains situated in front of the Moorish Palacio de la Almudaina (*see* Honderos *box, p34*).
At the end of the gardens walk through an

Modernista decor in Carrer de Jaume II

arch and cross the small garden in Plaça de la Reina.

7 Passeig des Born

Walk the length of this historic avenue (*see pp44–5*).
Turn right into Carrer de l'Unió.

8 Plaça Weyler

Passing the shabby bulk of the Circule de Belles Arts on your left, and the leafy world of Plaça del Mercat (*see p45*) on the right, you reach Plaça Weyler and the Modernista grandeur of the Fundació La Caixa (*see p38*). Follow the curve of the road, passing the Teatre Principal, to reach the tree-lined avenue of La Rambla, which was once a river but is today awash with flower stalls.
Climb up Costa de la Pols, by the Libreria Fondevilas bookshop, to return to Carrer de Sant Miquel.

Walk: Maritime Palma

Palma embraces the sea, and a stroll along its waterfront provides ample proof that this long-standing love affair is far from over. This easy walk follows the curve of the bay from the city centre to its passenger ship terminal, and is particularly enjoyable in the early evening. It can also be done in reverse – just take a taxi, a number 1 bus, or a horse-drawn carriage out to the Estació Marítimo, and walk back. (*See map on pp32–3 for route.*)
Allow 1½ hours one way.

The walk starts in Passeig de Sagrera, just west of the roundabout and statue of

Ramón Llull at the southern end of Avinguda d'Antoni Maura.

1 Passeig de Sagrera
Lined with tall palms, this pedestrian avenue is flanked to the north by historic buildings recalling Palma's maritime past. An ancient gate to the port, Porta Vella del Moll, has been reconstructed to the left of the 15th-century Exchange, La Llotja (*see p38*). Next door is the galleried Consulat del Mar, built in the 17th century as a court to resolve trading disputes. Decorated with flags and cannons, it is now used by the Balearic Islands' government.

Two statues can be seen at either end of Passeig de Sagrera. To the east is the bearded medieval sage Ramón Llull, apparently making notes of traffic violations with pen and quill. To the west is the Nicaraguan writer and modernist poet Rubén Dario.
Cross Avinguda Gabriel Roca by the yellow traffic lights and walk west along the seafront.

The main entrance to La Llotja

2 Port de Pesca

Lines of vivid blue nets strung along the quayside mark the entrance to Palma's fishing port, where fishermen paint boats and mend nets. The monumental pair of sundials nearby offers a brainteasing explanation of how to convert True Time into Legal Time.
Continue walking west, passing through a small garden.

3 Passeig Marítim

Though bordered by a busy road, this waterside promenade allows walkers to progress peacefully round the harbour. A 4.5-km cycle track from Portixol west to Sa Pedrera runs alongside. On the left you pass Palma's Reial Club Nautic (Royal Yacht Club), while across the road rise the mighty bastions that once protected Palma. The remains of five windmills dominate the skyline. On the horizon ahead you can see the imposing silhouette of Castell de Bellver. Further along you reach a tree-lined jetty where excursion boats offer tours of the harbour, and a monument celebrates Palma's 15th-century cartographers.
Continue west along the seafront.

4 Club de Mar

This walk is really a social climb through Palma's seafaring classes. Hardworking fishing vessels give way to hobby boats and weekend craft, rust buckets and tourist galleons are overshadowed by gin palaces and Mediterranean cruise ships. The Club de Mar is where many of these pleasure boats moor – a captivating sight for anyone drawn to the romance of the sea. Spare a moment to look back across the bay at Palma cathedral.

Working fishing boats add a note of salty realism to the leisured ambience of Palma's seafront

Follow the pavement east, passing under a bridge.

5 Estació Marítimo

Naval ships, cruise liners, ferries from mainland Spain and the other Balearic islands all call here at various times of the year. Walk as far as the large anchor set on a lawn, and you can see two more signs of Palma's maritime prowess: the 15th-century Torre Paraires, like a chess-piece castle, and beyond it the medieval lighthouse at Porto Pi.
Take a taxi or number 1 bus back from Estació Marítimo 2.

West of Palma

The western corner of Mallorca was one of the first areas to be settled by the Spanish in the 13th century – a cross at Santa Ponça commemorates the spot where Jaume I and his troops landed on 12 September 1229. Today a ribbon of resorts decorates the south coast all the way to Sant Telm, the port closest to the dramatic, lizard-shaped island of Sa Dragonera. Inland, and along the precipitous north coast, you can tour some of the most enjoyable mountain scenery on the island.

CASTELL DE BENDINAT

The outline of this 13th-century castle can easily be seen 8km west of Palma, near the turn-off for Bendinat when you are driving along the Palma–Andratx road. Enlarged in the 18th century, Castell de Bendinat is now a conference hall and not open to the public, but nevertheless makes a majestic sight with its battlements, fortified towers and surrounding pinewoods. According to an oft-told story, its name derives from an after-dinner remark uttered by a contented Jaume I after the king and his retinue had dined on the site in 1229. 'Havem ben dinat' ('We have eaten well'), the monarch declared.

Andratx

Known to the Romans as *Andrachium*, Andratx was built inland from its harbour (Port d'Andratx) as a precaution against pirate attack, a measure that has also saved it from the tourism developments now ravaging this coast. Framed by orange groves, the town appears still to be on the defensive, with sturdy buildings lining its narrow streets, its few shops hiding their minimal wares behind opaque doors and curtained windows. Andratx is dominated by the hulking 13th-century church of Santa Maria, which was rebuilt in the 1720s, and – further up the

Scene on the Victory Cross at Santa Ponça

valley – the castellated 16th-century mansion of Son Mas.

32km west of Palma on the C719. Tourist Office: Avenida de la Cúria, 1. Tel: (971) 62 80 00.

Cala Major

The Badia de Palma is fringed with a string of tourist developments of which Cala Major is the closest to Palma. The resort is a mixture of high-class residences now somewhat swamped by mass-market complexes. There is a small sandy beach but parking can be difficult.

Further west are two more resorts, **Sant Agusti** and **Ses Illetes**, with similar facilities. The latter has a less frantic atmosphere, with swimming possible off the rocks. The three resorts are fast becoming one, though who is devouring who is uncertain.

The coastline here is dominated by the closely-guarded summer residence of the Spanish royal family at Marivent, where the monarchs indulge in their favourite pastimes of sailing and entertaining.

6km west of Palma.

West of Palma *(see pp64–5 for route)*

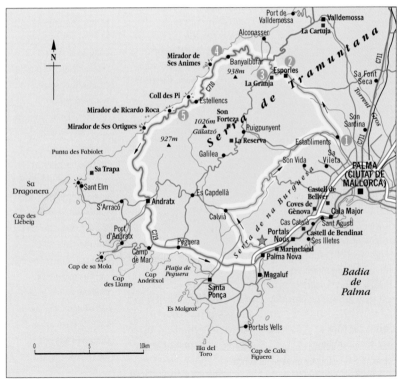

Calvià

On the southern edge of the Serra de Tramuntana, Calvià appears to be just another attractive country town where nothing much happens. But as the administrative centre for the district of Calvià, its municipal offices rule over a great swathe of pulsating resorts stretching west from Ses Illetes to Santa Ponça. Despite the profits and problems this brings, the town remains endearingly tranquil, with rustic bars and Mallorcan-cuisine restaurants where you can escape the madness of the coast. Calvià's unmissable landmark is its church, begun in 1245. The small square beside it offers extensive views over the neighbouring farms and fields flecked with olive and carob trees. Don't miss the lively pictorial history of the town displayed in tiles on the wall of the nearby library.

18km west of Palma, take the road to Establiments. Tourist Office: Calle Puig de Galatzó. Tel: (971) 69 17 12.

Camp de Mar

In a secluded bay surrounded by high cliffs, this holiday village has a small sandy beach with swimming off the rocks. Just offshore is a tiny islet reached by a frail bridge, where there is a restaurant. An enjoyable 5km walk leads uphill from Camp de Mar, west along a coast of fine views and fragant pines, and down again to Port d'Andratx (*see pp60–61*).

25km west of Palma, 4km east of Peguera.

Coves de Gènova

Nature appears to have created the Coves de Gènova for the convenience of visitors staying in the Palma area. If you don't have the time or inclination to see the great multicoloured caverns at Artà, Drac and Hams (*see p99, p121 & p124*), these caves offer a brief insight into the wonderland of stalactites and stalagmites that lies just below the surface of Mallorca. They are located close to several good restaurants – the entrance is in the grounds of Restaurant Servei and tickets for the guided tour are sold at the bar.

5km west of Palma. Look for signs to Gènova off the Palma–Andratx motorway, then climb up a steep hill to

MUSHROOMS

In the Mallorcan countryside you may see signs declaring '*Se Prohibe Buscar Setas*' (No Picking Mushrooms). The warnings are worth heeding, not because you might be pinching an islander's breakfast, but because it is hard for the untrained eye to tell the difference between the edible and the poisonous. Some 700 species are found on Mallorca, including four or five that can be deadly. Wild mushrooms are generally picked in the autumn – look for the trumpet-shaped *girgola* variety sold in markets.

the Coves. Carrer de Barranc 45.
Tel: (971) 40 23 87. Open: daily
10am–1.30pm, 4–7pm (summer);
10.30am–1pm, 4–6pm (winter).
Admission charge. Bus: 4.

Fundació Pilar i Joan Miró

In Spanish eyes, the artist Joan Miró is
nothing less than a saint. The hillside
house and purpose-built studio where
the painter lived and worked from 1956
has now been proclaimed 'Miró
Territory'. Galleries have been built in
bleached stone to exhibit some of the
5,000 works he left behind, and you can
peep into the studio where he worked,
left much as it was at the time of his
death in 1983. The adjacent garden, with
its trees, stones and old cartwheel, gives
clues to the way Miró drew inspiration
from the Mallorcan landscape. As his
friend Joan Prats put it: 'When I pick up
a rock it's a rock; when Miró picks it up,
it's a Miró.'

4km from Palma. Bus: 3, 4 & 21. Carrer
de Joan de Saridakis 29, Cala Major.
Tel: (971) 70 14 20. Open: 16 May–15
Sept, Tue–Sat 10am–7pm; 16 Sept–15
May, Tue–Sat 10am–6pm, Sun 10am–3pm
year round. Admission charge.

The story of Calvià's agriculture is recorded in tiles on the walls of the town library

Galilea

If you get the urge to jump into a hire car and swap the concrete mayhem of the Badia de Palma for tranquil rural scenery and the mountain air, Galilea is a worthwhile destination. You can get to this isolated village via Calvià (*see p54*) or Puigpunyent (*see p62*), following winding but generally quiet roads through delightful scenery. To the north rises the mighty peak of Puig de Galatzó.

Surrounded by cultivated hills with almond and carob trees and the odd picturesque windmill, Galilea has developed into an artists' colony. Steep roads lead up to the parish church in Plaça Pio XII, from where there are terrific views down the island to the sea. Two restaurants make a visit here complete.

25km west of Palma, 13km north of Calvià.

Hort de Palma (Garden of Palma)

On the northwestern outskirts of Palma is the fertile countryside called Hort de Palma. This cultivated landscape, with its small villages and undulating roads, is only 5km from the centre of the capital and makes a refreshing change from the resorts below. Several old estates and mansions have been turned into high-class hotels and restaurants.

From the Palma–Andratx motorway or the Via Cintura ring road, follow the signs north for Son Vida, passing through the busy shopping district of Sa Vileta. The Hotel Son Vida, a converted castle, and the newer Arabella Golf Hotel, with gardens and golf courses, are two luxury hotels. Open to non-residents, they make a refined venue for a drink or meal.

La Granja

A grand Mallorcan country house set on

The mansion of La Granja

and a parade of luxury villas climbing up the hillside. The port is a favourite haunt of the yachting fraternity. In summer, boat excursions run to the nearby island of Sa Dragonera *(see p140).*
35km west of Palma, 5km south of Andratx.

Portals Nous

Portals Nous is an upmarket tourist complex with a small sandy beach, and swimming off the rocks. At its eastern end is Porto Portals, a top-notch marina opened in 1987 that attracts fabulously expensive yachts and cruisers. If you like mixing with the well-tanned well-off, and enjoy promenading past ships' chandlers and boutiques selling designer nautical gear, this is the place for you. There is a good choice of ritzy restaurants, with cuisines ranging from *nouvelle* to Chinese. Behind this opulent shore, high-walled villas sit among the pines, and barking dogs warn that you are on moneyed ground.
10km west of Palma off the PM1 motorway, or the C719.

Porto Portals, where the rich moor up

Portals Vells

A left turn off the Palma–Andratx road, signposted Cala Figuera, leads south past a golf course and thick pinewoods to the western horn of the Badia de Palma. A turning left down a dusty side road can take you to the tiny but official nudist beach at Platja Mago, where there is a small beach bar.

Continuing south you reach the small bay of Cala de Portals Vells. Walk along the south side of the cliffs and you will reach the Cove de la Mare de Déu, a rock church with two altars and elaborate rock carvings. Legend has it that Genoese fishermen sheltering from a storm placed a statue of the Virgin from their ship in the caves as a thanks-offering for their survival. In 1866 the statue was taken to the chapel on the seafront in Portals Nous.

In the 13th and 14th centuries the caves were quarried to supply stone for Palma cathedral. The peninsula is also used by the military.
24km southwest of Palma.

Puigpunyent

Tucked into a valley, Puigpunyent is a pretty village you will inevitably pass through if you are touring the interior of the western Serra de Tramuntana. Nearby are the historic country house La Granja, the splendid nature reserve La Reserva and the epic road to Galilea (*see p56 & p138*).

Two kilometres along the road north to Esporles is the 17th-century mansion house Son Fortesa, a typical Mallorcan country estate with waterfalls and citrus orchards. Prince Charles spent a holiday sketching here in 1991.

The Gran Hotel Son Net and L'Orangerie Restaurant offer sheer elegance and luxury.
15km northwest of Palma, 8km west of Establiments.

Santa Ponça

Just west of the Badia de Palma, this sheltered resort is on an attractive site, with pinewoods and a large sandy beach washed by clear, shallow water. Often used by British tour operators, it is packed in summer, but never attains the brash atmosphere of nearby Magaluf. A marina, golf course and water-sports are part of its wide-ranging facilities.

A cross commemorates the victory of the Catalan troops over the Moors

THE CONQUEST OF MALLORCA

Jaume I's original plan was to land his troops in the Badia de Pollença, but a storm forced his fleet along the island's north coast to Sant Telm. He came well armed, with 150 ships carrying 16,000 troops and 1,500 horses. The Moors fled to the mountains, and Palma was besieged for three months before its surrender on 31 December 1229. By the following March, the king was rewarding his conquistadores with huge estates.

Caleta de Santa Ponça

From the marina, a road signposted Sa Caleta leads south to the rocky headland of Es Malgrat. En route you will reach a superb vantage point, Caleta de Santa Ponça, site of a large white Victory Cross, a memorial erected in 1929 to mark the 700th anniversary of the landing on Mallorca of Jaume I of Aragón on 12 September 1229.

In the battle that morning some 1,500 Moors were killed. Sculpted scenes depict the bravery of the Christian troops.

Further along the same road, after passing many substantial villas, is a spot from where you can look back towards Santa Ponça, enjoying the sea air and a panoramic view. You will also see fishermen who appear to like sitting perilously on the cliff-edge with their long rods.

Out at sea lie the craggy islands of Illa Malgrat and Illa na Fordada, and further west the headlands of Cap Andritxol and Cap des Llamp.

Santa Ponça is 20km west of Palma on the C719. Tourist Office: Puig de Galatzó. Tel: (971) 69 17 12.

Santa Ponça's marina

Tour: West of Palma

You do not have to drive far from Palma or its neighbouring resorts to enjoy the peace of Mallorca's countryside. This 86-km circular trip guides you round the mountains to the northwest of Palma, climbing along winding rural roads to reach the spectacular cliffs and sea views of the north coast. (*See p53 for route.*)

Allow 5 hours.

The tour begins at Palma Nova, 5km west of Palma on the PM1 motorway or C719.

1 Establiments

Take the PM1015 north, following signs to Calvià. The high-rise buildings of the coast are soon replaced by woods and well-tended farmland, and the twin spires of Calvià's church can be seen in the distance. In the centre of this town (*see p54*), turn right at a T-junction in the direction of Establiments. Climbing steadily, you pass several grand country houses with wrought-iron gates guarding their entrances. The small village of Establiments is where George Sand and Chopin first stayed during their visit of 1838–9, amid a landscape she considered worthy of Poussin's paintbrush.

From Establiments, take the left turn to Esporles.

Terrace view: working the fields in Banyalbufar

2 Esporles

Sheltered by high mountain ridges, this pretty town of tree-lined streets makes a pleasant place to stop for a drink or lunch. Apples, pears, oranges and figs, grown on the terraces surrounding Esporles, are sold in its shops.
Continue north following the signs to Banyalbufar and La Granja.

3 La Granja

La Granja (*see pp56–7*) offers a rare chance to enter one of the highly covetable *fincas* (country houses) that adorn the interior of Mallorca. Today it is a folk museum.
Continue north to join the C710, turning left for Banyalbufar.

4 Banyalbufar

The sinuous drive along this coast provides magnificent views of mountains, terraced slopes, high cliffs and the sea far below. Clinging perilously to a narrow ridge is the small village of Banyalbufar. Some of the buildings lining its narrow main street are supported by stilts. A few shops and hotels cater to visitors seeking an away-from-it-all holiday. A steep, winding road leads down to the tiny port.
Continue west through Estellencs.

5 Miradores

The steep terraces along here, which support thriving crops of tomatoes, grapes and flowers, were originally constructed by the Moors and are still worked mostly by hand. Several viewpoints (*miradores*) provide a chance to stop and take in the impressive coastline. At the first, **Mirador de Ses**

Coastal watchtower at the Mirador de Ses Animes, just south of Banyalbufar

Animes, is a restored watchtower built on a high rock beside the cliffs (which can be climbed). If this is crowded, you can continue on through Estellencs to a second *mirador* at **Coll des Pi**, where you will find refreshments and a petrol station, and a good view inland to **Puig de Galatzó** (1,026m).

The parish church at **Estellencs** dates from 1422, and a tortuous road leads down to a small cove with a rocky beach. Further southwest are more viewpoints: **Mirador de Ricardo Roca**, which has a large restaurant, and **Mirador de Ses Ortigues**.
The road descends comfortably through fields studded with olives to the stately old town of Andratx (see pp52–3). A 5km detour can be made from here down to Port d'Andratx (see pp60–61), where there is a good choice of harbourside restaurants. From Andratx it is a simple 13km drive east along the fast PM1 or C719 to Palma Nova.

Walk: Sa Trapa

Hidden away in the cliffs north of Sant Telm is the abandoned Trappist monastery of Sa Trapa: it will linger long in your memory if you make the effort to get there. The best route provides superb views over the island of Sa Dragonera, but involves some scrambling up steep rocks. If you prefer, you can get there and return by an inland cart track, as the monks surely did. The track is well signposted. Take a light picnic.

Allow 3 hours return, excluding time at Sa Trapa.

The small resort of Sant Telm lies 8km west of Andratx and is connected by bus to Palma via Peguera. There is a frequent service to Andratx, and you can take a taxi to Sant Telm from the rank beside the Teatro Argentino there. If you are driving, park by the start of the walk at the northern end of Sant Telm in Plaça de

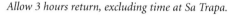

Mosser Sebastià Grau – where there is a blue-and-white windmill.

1 Sant Telm

Follow the shore along Avinguda Jaume I and Carrer Cala en Basset, bearing right into Plaça de Mosser Sebastià Grau. Take Avinguda de la Trapa inland; it becomes a country track through pinewoods to the Can Tomeví farmhouse. Here a sign directs you right for Sa Trapa, passing behind the house. At the next sign, Sa Font des Moros, you have a choice – turn left for a steep ascent of the cliffs, or continue straight on to follow the easier but longer inland track up to Sa Trapa (380m), also the return route.

2 The Ascent

Turning left, walk through the woods until you reach a pair of small concrete gateposts. Turn right here, marked on a nearby stone by the first of many small intermittent black paint arrows that lead the way. The path narrows as it climbs through the trees, crossing several walls and passing the stone ruins of a limekiln. Eventually you ascend above the pines, with ever-improving views of craggy Sa Dragonera just offshore. After a short scramble up through dwarf palms and over steep, bare rocks, you will meet a well-established path that makes an ascending run north through the trees.

Passing a '280' in blue paint, you reach a clifftop viewpoint – a good place to take a breather and admire the coast-line below. Continue to follow the path as marked, taking care on the final ascent which nears the cliff-edge – heed the warning crosses and veer right. Suddenly you are on top of the promontory, and can see the romantic buildings of Sa Trapa in the valley ahead.

3 Sa Trapa

Follow the path to the monastery, a formidable ensemble, where you can wander round the ruined chapel,

kitchen and living quarters. Almond trees continue to blossom on its perfectly-built terraces, the mill still has its ancient machinery, and you can easily make out the wide sweep of the threshing floor, now punctured by pines that have grown up since the monastery's closure in the late 18th century. A memorial stone nearby is a sad reminder to keep away from the cliff-edge here.

4 The Descent

Sa Trapa is now being restored and conserved by the Grupo Ornithologia Balear (GOB) and the track used by their vehicles offers an easy descent. This leads inland from behind the monastery, climbs over a pass, then winds patiently down the mountainside, providing ample time to dwell upon the life of this isolated Trappist community. At the bottom the track crosses a bridge, curves through a farm and – forking right – leads down to the house at Can Tomeví.

A boat from Sant Telm will take you to Sa Dragonera, the island with steep sides

The Northwest

Served by Mallorca's two railway lines, this is both the most accessible part of the island and the best place to get a taste of Mallorca as it was before the resorts arrived. Besides being a spectacular mountain range, the Serra de Tramuntana is full of secrets. Take the slow train up to Sóller, make the hairy descent to Sa Calobra, pay a visit to the monasteries at Valldemossa and Lluc, and you will have a completely different image of Mallorca.

A corner of the garden at Alfabia

Alfabia

The gardens of Alfabia are a delightful memento of when Mallorca was under Moorish rule. Then the estate was known as Al-Fabi ('jar of olives' in Arabic), a lofty residence fit for *viziers* (high-ranking officials) where the Arab talent for irrigation, garden design and horticulture flourished. The estate is an inviting oasis where you can spend a dreamy morning or afternoon in the shade of swaying palms and fragrant flowers.

An avenue of magisterial plane trees guides visitors to the stone archway marking the entrance. Follow the directions to walk to the left of the house and up steps to the gardens. Cobbled paths lead past a huge cistern and water channels to a long pergola wreathed with a colourful mix of begonia, bougainvillaea, wisteria and honeysuckle. Lavender, sage and box form low hedges, while tall date palms and exotic shrubs provide shaded walks accompanied by the soothing tune of flowing water. At a lower level there are ponds with lilies and fish, bamboos, twining subtropical plants and groves of lemon and orange trees in side gardens.

The house and gardens at Alfabia, a retreat from the summer heat since Moorish times

Tours (see pp86–7 for orange tour, pp88–9 for green tour)

The house, though somewhat run-down, is a fascinating relic of bygone days, with faded wall panels and antique furniture – look out for the 14th-century carved wooden chair, and an ancient cradle.

14km north of Palma on the C711. Tel: (971) 61 31 23. Open: Apr–Sept, Mon–Fri 9.30am–6.30pm, Sat 9.30am–6pm; Oct–Mar, Mon–Fri 9.30am–5.30pm. Closed: Sun. Admission charge.

Binissalem

Binissalem is the centre of Mallorca's wine-making industry. Viticulture was introduced to the islands by the Romans and survived the Moorish occupation (Binissalem means 'House of Salem' in Arabic). Production reached a peak in the late 19th century when blight struck the French vineyards. Then there were 30,000 hectares under vines; today, that's down to 400, but the reputation of Mallorcan wines is growing with the help of modern technology and grape varieties exclusive to the island. Wine can be bought from the Bodega José Ferrer (minimum purchase, six bottles). For the El Foro de Mallorca wax museum, *see p157*.
22km northeast of Palma on the C713.

Castell d'Alaró

There is little reason to linger in the

The island's best wine comes from Binissalem

village of Alaró, except on a Friday afternoon when you might buy picnic provisions in the market prior to ascending to the nearby Castell d'Alaró (817m). To reach this romantically sited castle, drive northeast on the PM210 towards Orient. At km18, a turning left leads on to a narrow road bordered by stone walls and fields of olives and almond trees. This degenerates into a rough dirt track full of potholes, best suited to four-wheel drive vehicles or hikers with sturdy footwear.

An alternative approach is to continue skirting right round Puig d'Alaró, park near km11, then follow a path up through the terraces. Either way, you eventually reach a high plateau where your perseverance is rewarded with fantastic views, and Es Pouet, a rustic bar-restaurant that serves delicious roast lamb cooked in a clay oven. From here, you must walk (30 minutes) up steep and winding stone steps to see the ruins of the 15th-century castle. A small chapel, **Mare de Déu del Refugi**, has stood here since 1622 and a hostelry still offers sanctuary to pilgrims and visitors.
29km northeast of Palma, 6km north of Alaró. Right-of way dispute: check route with Aguntament d'Alaro (tel: (971) 51 00 00), or the Castel (tel: (971) 18 21 12).

Costitx

Typical of the many small towns in the interior of Mallorca, Costitx was the main centre of population on the island in prehistoric times, and the area has proved a rich source of archaeological treasures. The 14th-century image of the Virgin in its parish church is said to have been found by children in an apple tree.

The path up to the ruins of the 15th-century Castell d'Alaró – fine views guaranteed

Casa de Sa Fauna Ibero-Balear

This modern building lies on the south side of the main road from Costitx to Sencelles, signposted Casa Cultura. It exhibits stuffed and preserved examples of the fauna of the Balearic Islands, including wild birds, fish and butterflies. There is a bar-restaurant and library, and a good view of the surrounding agricultural plains.

Can Font. Tel: (971) 51 31 98.
Open: Tue–Sat 9.30am–1pm.
Closed: Mon & 1st & 3rd Sun of the month. Admission charge.

Costitx is 24km northeast of Palma, 4.5km east of Sencelles.

Coves de Campanet

Campanet is a quiet old town, devoid of tourism and peaceful even on market day. Just 3km to the north, though, the Coves de Campanet are a magnet for sightseers and excursion coaches. Discovered in 1945, the caves are not as spectacular as those at Artà, Drac or Hams (*see p99, p121 & p124*), but neither are they as crowded with visitors. The well-signposted entrance is through a colourful garden dripping with bougainvillaea and other flamboyant plants, and a large terrace provides a rewarding opportunity to sit with a drink and survey the charming rural scenery in the Sant Miquel Valley.

Conducted tours lead visitors into a subterranean maze that winds for some 1,300m past colourfully illuminated stalactites and stalagmites and 'The Enchanted Town'.

41km northeast of Palma, 12km northwest of Inca. Tel: (971) 51 61 30.
Open: daily, Apr–Sept 10am–7pm; Oct–Mar 10am–6pm. Admission charge.

The landscaped entrance to the subterranean caves at Campanet

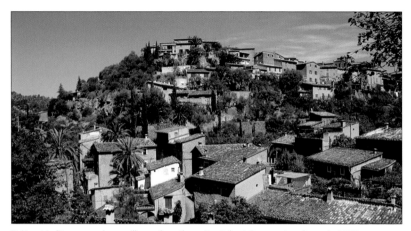

Deià: a Mediterranean dream village where the writer Robert Graves set up home in 1929

Deià

Lodged amid the mountains of the north coast, Deià will be forever associated with the English writer, Robert Graves, who came to live here in 1929 and developed a deep affection for Mallorca and its people. He is buried in the cemetery beside the parish church at the top of the town. Graves strove hard to stop Deià being ruined by the encroaching tourist developments: the town's unified and natural appearance is its greatest attraction. There are several restaurants, a couple of art galleries and a narrow, twisting road that leads down to the sea at Cala de Deià.

Many foreign residents now live in and around Deià, and rising property prices have changed its atmosphere. Today, the town lives in thrall to La Residencia, an idyllic mansion turned hotel that was formerly owned by British entrepreneur Richard Branson and attracts the very rich and famous from around the world. As author Robert Elms put it, 'Everything in Deià is taken slowly, except your money.' *30km north of Palma, 4km south of Lluc-Alcari.*

Fornalutx

This is a truly pretty mountain village with a narrow cobbled high street that twists round to a tiny square. The church dates from 1680. Several cafés and inviting restaurants, such as the Santa Marta with its terrace views, make Fornalutx a welcome goal if you are walking from Sóller. Follow the rural road east via Biniaraix, through a valley graced with orange and lemon groves. *40km north of Palma, 8km northeast of Sóller via the C710 to Lluc or 5km via Biniaraix.*

Inca

On the railway line from Palma, this modern industrial town is heavily promoted as a place all tourists should visit. Excursions are arranged to the

Thursday outdoor market, which spreads around the streets bordering the covered daily market, and usually include a visit to one of the town's several leather factories or their retail outlets along Avinguda General Luque and Gran Via de Colon. Prices are not so low as to merit a special trip, but there is plenty of choice.

Pursuers of Mallorcan cuisine will appreciate the *celler* restaurants in the town centre, where the wine is extracted from mammoth vats, and you can join the locals devouring local specialities such as *caracoles* (snails) and roast suckling pig. Can Amer in Carrer den Miquel Durán is a famous example. In the shops you may see *concos d'Inca* ('Inca bachelors') for sale, a type of cake made by the nuns of Monasterio de las Jerónimas. The island's top agricultural show is held here on the third Thursday in November and is known as Dijous Bò – Good Thursday.

Ermita de Santa Magdalena

A turning right off the Inca-Alcúdia road leads up to Puig d'Inca (304m) and a small sanctuary looking over the countryside and mountains. There is a small chapel and a café. A pilgrimage, said to have been followed for 800 years, is made every year to the *ermita* on the first Sunday after Easter.

Inca is 30km northeast of Palma on the C713.

Robert Graves
English poet and novelist Robert Graves (1895–1985) is well known for his two bestsellers: *Goodbye to All That,* an autobiographical account of his experiences in World War I, and *I, Claudius,* a historical novel that brings to life ancient Rome. Money made from the first book enabled him to move to Mallorca with his muse, mistress and fellow poet Laura Riding. After World War II he settled permanently on the island, writing fiction, poetry and books on mythology.

The peaceful central square in Fornalutx, a mountain village surrounded by citrus groves

Creative Mallorca

Mallorca has stimulated the creativity of many visiting writers, musicians and artists. George Sand was

convinced that the sublimity of Chopin's *Preludes*, composed or completed during their stay at Valldemossa in 1838–9, was a direct response to an environment enriched by deceased monks, birds singing in wet trees and the twang of far-off guitars. To her mind, raindrops falling on the Charterhouse roof were transformed by Chopin's 'imagination and singing gift into tears falling on the heart'. Chopin denied that his art was achieved by a puerile imitation of the external, but critics agree that he emerged from his Mallorcan sojourn a more mature composer.

Painter and sculptor Joan Miró, whose mother and wife came from Mallorca, was more candid about the direct

influence of the island on his vibrantly-coloured work. 'As a child,' he recalled, 'I loved to watch the always changing Mallorcan sky. At night I would get carried away by the writing in the sky of the shooting stars, and the lights of the fireflies. The sea, day and night, was always blue. It was here that I received the first creative seeds which became my work.' Miró's studio on the outskirts of Palma is a testimony to the way the artist found inspiration in nature's little works – a piece of driftwood, an almond stone, a dry-stone wall 'carved by real masters'.

The minutiae of island life also absorbed the writer and long-term Deià-resident Robert Graves, whose *Majorcan Stories* chronicle tragicomic vicissitudes befalling both locals and visitors, such as the bicycle theft or a farcical christening.

The greatest and most diligent creative response to Mallorca, however, must be the work of the indefatigable Archduke Luis Salvador. Arriving on the island in 1867 at the age of 19, he sank his fortune into researching his beloved island, sponsoring investigations of its caves and archaeological sites and producing a comprehensive six-volume study of the Balearic Islands, *Die Balearen*, that is still valued to this day.

Among those inspired by the vibrant beauty of Mallorca were Chopin (above and facing page below) and Joan Miró (facing page above) whose studio outside Palma is open to visitors

The monastery at Lluc has grown from humble 13th-century origins into a monumental complex

Lluc

A revered place of pilgrimage since its founding in 1250, the Monestir de Lluc (Monastery of Lluc) is a testimony to the Mallorcans' continuing religious conviction. Legend has it that a shepherd boy discovered an image of a dark-skinned Virgin in the forest here and took it to the local priest. The Virgin was placed in the village church at Escorca, but disappeared three times, always being found in the same spot in the forest. Taking this as a divine command, the priest ordered the construction of a chapel to house the peripatetic Virgin.

Today, Lluc is a colossal ensemble that includes a church, choir school, the old Augustinian monastery, a small museum, accommodation for pilgrims and a restaurant and souvenir shop for visitors. To reach the church, enter the main building by the front portal,

following a short passage past a patio with a magnificent magnolia to a courtyard. To the right is the Baroque façade of the church. Inside, steps lead up behind the altar to a chapel and the jewel-adorned image of La Moreneta, the Little Dark One, who is Mallorca's patron saint. You can hear the choirboys – known as Els Blavets (The Blues) from the colour of their cassocks – at the 11.15am service. The museum, on the first floor, contains a miscellany of thanksgiving gifts, archaeological finds, coins, costumes and paintings. To the left of the monastery buildings is a path leading to a Way of the Cross, with good views of the quiet countryside. The sculptures, depicting the Mysteries of the Rosary, are the work of the Modernista architects Antoni Gaudí and Joan Rubió, who undertook modernisation of the church at Lluc. Several mountain walks start from here.

The cafés in Plaça Constitució, Sóller, are just the place to watch the world not go by

Greek temple in white marble where the Archduke would sit and contemplate the sea and the mountains.

The rocky headland below, called Sa Foradada, is pierced by an 18-m wide hole. You can walk down to the landing stage, built so that the Archduke and his guests could moor their yachts and swim off the rocks. Ask for permission from the house before you set off.

33km north of Palma, 4km west of Deià on the C710. Tel: (971) 63 91 58.
Open: daily 9.30am–2pm, 3–7.30pm (5.30pm between Nov & Mar).
Admission charge.

The Archduke

Archduke Luis Salvador (1847–1915) was a wealthy member of the Austrian imperial family who first set eyes on Mallorca while yachting round the Mediterranean. An ardent naturalist, he spent a great part of his life on the island and owned several estates on the northwest coast in addition to Son Marroig. Stories of his scholastic endeavour are frequently spiced with gossip about his affair with a local girl stricken by leprosy, and every islander has an Archduke story to tell. One recalls how a farmer, unaware of who he was dealing with, gave him a few coins in reward for helping him shift some barrels. 'That is the first money I have earned in my life,' quipped the Archduke.

Mallorca is still reeling from the visit paid to the island in 1838 by the French literary celebrity George Sand and her lover, Polish composer Frédéric Chopin. Sand, the *nom de plume* of Baroness Amandine Aurore Lucie Dupin (1804–76), was also accompanied by her 14-year-old son, Maurice, and eight-year-old daughter, Solange.

In those days there was little accommodation for foreigners available on the island. The party stayed first in a villa in Establiments, but were forced to move out when rumours spread among the villagers that Chopin had tuberculosis, a disease from which he eventually died in 1849. A new home was found in three cells in the former Carthusian monastery at Valldemossa, just three years after its monks had been expelled. Their stay here was far from idyllic, characterised by poor food, 'lugubrious rain', Chopin's declining health and ostracism by the locals.

A free-thinking, cigarette-smoking, trouser-wearing pioneer feminist, Sand later commented how different things might have been had they bothered to attend Mass.

Mallorca has never forgiven Sand for the opinionated account of her travels given in *Un Hiver à Majorque* (A Winter in Majorca), published in 1842. While references to the islanders as thieves, monkeys and Polynesian savages are distasteful, her book is appreciative of the Mallorcan countryside and provides a memorable glimpse of the island just 150 years ago. Somewhat ironically, Sand and Chopin's visit has contributed to the image of Mallorca as an island of romance and cultural pedigree, and her book is now sold in several languages in Valldemossa. The English translation by Robert Graves includes his own idiosyncratic annotations. As he observed, the whole episode was a fascinating clash of the classical and romantic worlds.

Reial Cartoixa Chopin Festival

Each August (and occasionally during the rest of the year) a festival celebrates the music of Frederick Chopin with a series of Sunday concerts featuring his music. Performed by well-known and rising musicians, these are held in the Carthusian monastery at Valldemossa, where Chopin stayed with George Sand. During the festival the monastery also has exhibits on the period and its art and philosophy. *Tel: (971) 61 21 06.*

The Carthusian monastery at Valldemossa

Valldemossa

Valldemossa is associated with two women utterly different from each other. One is George Sand, the writer-feminist who spent the 1838–9 winter with lover Frédéric Chopin (*see pp82–3*) in a Carthusian monastery, Reial Cartoixa, which looms over the pretty hillside town. The other is Santa Catalina Thomás, Mallorca's 16th-century saint, revered in every Valldemossa home.

Plaques outside every house pay homage to Santa Catalina Thomás

Walk down the hill to the parish church, though, and you will discover that Valldemossa is more concerned with remembering Santa Catalina Thomás. There is scarcely a house without a painted tile beside the front door asking for her protection. Take Carrer de Rectoria to the left of the church to see the tiny dwelling where she was born, now restored as a shrine.

Reial Cartoixa
(Royal Carthusian Monastery)

The monastery (La Cartuja in Spanish) at Valldemossa developed from a royal palace given to the Carthusian order in 1399. Most of the buildings date from the 18th century when the community was at its most wealthy. Visitors enter through the gloomy Neo-Classical church, begun in 1751 and decorated with frescoes by Bayeu, Goya's brother-in-law. You walk into huge whitewashed cloisters, where signs point out a circuit of the rooms and cells where the monks lived. Their quarters seem luxurious compared to the popular conception of monastic life, with individual prayer rooms, fireplaces and vegetable gardens overlooking the valley.

The monks prepared and dispensed medicine in the Pharmacy; after their expulsion in 1835, one remained to continue treating the villagers. Their cells were auctioned off one by one, and some are still used as private summer residences. The head of the monastery resided in the Prior's Cell, where you can see memorabilia associated with the library of Santa Catalina Thomás, and some of the instruments of flagellation used in penitential moments.

Cells 2 and 4 recreate the rooms occupied by Sand and Chopin, and contain the manuscript of *A Winter in Majorca* and the two pianos used by the composer. A Pleyel piano

SANTA VERGE CATALINA
QUE PER SEMPRE AL CEL REINAU
OMPLIU DE FE I DE PAU
LA VILA VALLDEMOSSINA

The Northeast (see pp112–3 for tour)

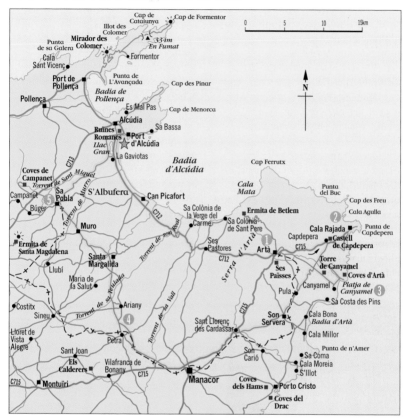

Old Town

Take the entrance to the old town next to the church of Sant Jaume, which stands at its southwestern corner. Before walking through, you can inspect some remnants of Roman houses lying just across the road behind a row of cypresses. The church of Sant Jaume dates from the 13th century, but the present building is mostly 19th century. On Sundays, it is tightly packed with worshippers.

To reach the town centre, walk along Carrer de Sant Jaume, turning left down Carrer dels Albellons. Turn right past Alcúdia's pompous Neo-Classical town hall to reach Plaça Constitució. Leave by the narrow shop-lined Carrer de Moll, which brings you to the massive Porta del Moll gate. To the right is Passeig de la Mare de Déu de La Victoria, where the town's market takes place on Thursday and Sunday. (See Tour pp112–3.)

Museu Monogràfic de Pollentia

Next to the church of Sant Jaume, this small museum is devoted to the history of Roman Pollentia.

Carrer de Sant Jaume 30.
Tel: (971) 54 70 04. Open: Apr–Sept,
Tue–Fri 10am–1.30pm & 3.30–5.30pm;
Oct–Mar, Tue–Fri 10am–1.30pm &
4–6pm, Sat–Sun 10.30am–1pm.
Closed: Mon. Admission charge.

Oratori de Sant Anna

Half a kilometre south of the town, on the road to Port d'Alcúdia, is a tiny chapel worth a visit purely for its simplicity and peaceful atmosphere. The oratory was built in the early 13th century and is believed to be Mallorca's oldest surviving church. Above the entrance is a carved statue of the Virgin Bona Nova.

The chapel is on the north side of
the road, opposite a cemetery.
Open: mornings only.

Ruines Romanes

A Roman amphitheatre stands 1.5km southwest of the town, on the right-hand side of the road to Port d'Alcúdia. It has the distinction of being the smallest Roman theatre in Spain, but all the same its tiered seats and stubby pillars carry a historic aura.

Open at all times.
Free admission.

Ermita de la Victoria

The peninsula northeast of Alcúdia can be visited by taking the road towards Es Mal Pas. Leave by the northern gate, Port Roja (near the bullring), and drive through the smart villas of Bonaire

The theatre at Alcúdia provides tangible evidence of the Roman presence on the island

toward Cap des Pinar. A watchtower, Torre Major, was constructed on its summit (451m) by Philip II in 1599. En route you will pass a turning to the right, which leads up to a fortress-like hermitage. Inside is a 15th-century wooden statue honouring Victoria, Alcúdia's patroness. Although the road to Cap des Pinar concludes in a military zone, much of this scenic headland is a nature reserve and a rewarding venue for walks, picnics or a cycle ride, offering attractive views.

55km northeast of Palma on the C713, 11km east of Pollença.

Artà

The spires and battlements of this medieval hilltop town can be seen from afar, and although Artà now has a bypass it is well worth a visit. Known to

the Moors as Jartan, Artà has an atmosphere of great antiquity that clearly emanates from its principal attraction, the Santuari de Sant Salvador. To reach this, follow signs to the centre of the town, then on and up to the sanctuary: this involves narrow streets, not always one-way. If you prefer a stiff, soul-enhancing climb, you can take the long, cypress-lined stone stairway that leads from the town centre up past the parish church of the Transfiguració del Senyor.

Tourist Office: Costa i Llobera, s/n (Antigua Estación de Tren). Tel: (971) 83 69 81.

Santuari de Sant Salvador

The sanctuary occupies the site of a Moorish fortress. The chapel and its castellated walls were built between 1825 and 1832, the previous hermitage having been knocked down as a counter-measure against the spread of a devastating plague. The views from its courtyard over Artà's terracotta roofs and the hazy countryside beyond are engrossing – take a bag of almonds and all your unwritten postcards.

Tel: (971) 82 72 82. Free admission to see grounds.

Museu Regional d'Artà

The museum displays archaeological finds such as ceramics, jewellery and bronzes from the nearby site of Ses Països (*see p110*) and elsewhere on the island.

Carrer d'Estrella 4. Tel: (971) 83 61 57. Open: Mon–Fri 10am–noon. Closed: Sat–Sun. Free admission.

Artà is 71km northeast of Palma on the C715.

Cala Sant Vicenç, a quiet resort protected by mountains and popular with artists

Cala Millor

Cala Millor is the epicentre of recent tourist-wooing developments along Mallorca's east coast. From Cap des Pinar south to Sa Coma, every little bay and cove appears to have sprouted a holiday complex. **Cap des Pinar**, named after the pines growing on this headland, endeavours to remain an upmarket enclave with luxury hotels and private villas. To the south in the Badia d'Artà is **Cala Bona**. Its role as a fishing port has been superseded with the addition of three man-made beaches and it is now a good spot for watersports, with several seafood restaurants.

Cala Millor is the largest and brashest resort, the coastline stacked with high-rise hotels and apartment blocks. Here the entertainment, like the beer, just keeps on coming – expect one long crowded party in summer. The beach has clean white sand and a wide promenade, with a good range of sports activities that include windsurfing, karting, bowling and riding. If you fancy a return to normality, walk into Son Servera for the Friday morning market.

An obstacle to the developers' projects is the protected headland at Punta de n'Amer. Just south is **Sa Coma**, another full-blown resort (but quieter than Cala Millor) with a great beach and tidy seafront. The roads here are reasonably flat and in good condition, making Sa Coma a good choice for an easy bike ride.

71km northeast of Palma, 15km south of Artà. Tourist offices in Cala Millor: Av. Joan Severa Camps, tel: (971) 58 58 64; Parc de la Mar 2, tel: (971) 58 54 09.

Cala Rajada

Another popular holiday resort that has evolved from a quiet fishing village, Cala Rajada possesses all the seaside amenities its international clientele expects, yet still retains some native Mallorcan charm. A one-way system leads visitors to the small harbour, where there is parking and a long promenade with shops and restaurants. The beaches close to the town are nothing special, but there are appealing sandy bays further north at Cala Guya, Cala Agulla and Cala Mesquida, and at Platja Son Moll to the south.

A 2-km walk uphill from the port, signposted Faro, leads through woodland to the breezy headland of Punta de Capdepera and its lighthouse.

Connoisseurs of modern art and gardens should consider visiting **Casa March**, a private estate which belongs to the wealthy March family. The grounds contain sculptures by Rodin, Henry Moore, Barbara Hepworth and several Spanish artists.

80km northeast of Palma, 3km east of Capdepera. Visits by appointment only through the local tourist office. Tourist office: Plaça dels Pins. Tel: (971) 56 30 33.

Cala Sant Vicenç

This secluded resort is tucked away in the northeast corner of the island. Its two sandy bays, sheltered by the Serra de Cornavaques to the west, and Serra de Cavall Bernat to the east, are divided by the San Pedro hotel, with a jumble of other hotels, restaurants and shops following the shoreline. Inland there are impressive villas with profusely flowering gardens. Cala Sant Vicenç, with its easygoing atmosphere and rugged cliff scenery, has always been an artists' haven: a statue on its promenade pays tribute to one local painter, Llorenc Cerda Bisbal.

56km northeast of Palma, 5km northeast of Pollença. Tourist Office: Plaça Cala Sant Vicenç, s/n. Tel: (971) 53 32 64.

Can Picafort

In the centre of the Badia d'Alcúdia, this fishing port turned resort has a good family beach fringed with low pines. A copious supply of restaurants, super-markets and souvenir shops meets the needs of visitors of all ages, who are mainly package holidaymakers staying in the high-rise hotels. Those who prefer quieter beaches and more solitude, should head north to Platja de Muro.

64km northeast of Palma, 11km southeast of Port d'Alcúdia. Tourist Office: Plaça Gabriel Roca 6. Tel: (971) 85 03 10. Open: Apr/May–Oct/Nov.

Sun-worship in Cala Millor

The Cap de Formentor peninsula offers clifftop viewpoints

Cap de Formentor

The peninsula of Cap de Formentor boasts some of Mallorca's most dramatic scenery, made accessible by a steep and winding road leading out to its isolated lighthouse. Leaving Port de Pollença, the road (PM221) climbs steadily with good views over the Badia de Pollença. Be sure to stop after 6km at the Mirador des Colomer, a breathtaking viewpoint above the sea-pounded cliffs. A small, rocky islet, Illot des Colomer, lies offshore and is a sanctuary for nesting seabirds.

From here the road narrows, with sharp bends where monster coaches love to hide. Two more small viewpoints conspire to exhaust your film stock, then the road drops down, passing a turning right for Platja de Formentor. Continue east along the spine of the peninsula for another 11km, passing through the En Fumat mountain to reach the lighthouse. This was built in 1860 and is closed to the public. Like many 'Land's Ends' around the world, Cap de Formentor can get ludicrously crowded, but few will dispute the magnificence of the sea views, which in good weather stretch to Menorca.

On the return trip, you might stop at Platja de Formentor, a beach visited by boat excursions from Port de Pollença in the summer, or call into the Hotel Formentor for a drink (suitable dress required). Tucked into the sheltered south coast of Cap de Formentor, the hotel was built in 1926 by the wealthy Argentinian Adan Dielh and helped put Mallorca on the luxury holiday map. *84km northeast of Palma, 20km northeast of Port de Pollença.*

Capdepera

Capdepera and its hilltop castle at the

Local history: Muro's ethnological museum

Museu Etnològic de Mallorca
The former town house of the Alomar family is now a museum devoted to Mallorcan traditions. There are comprehensive displays of rural furniture, local costume, agricultural tools and island crafts, including many examples of the Mallorcans' curious clay whistle known as the *siurell*.
Carrer Major 15. Tel: (971) 71 75 40. Open: Tue–Sat 10am–7pm; Sun 10am– 2pm. Closed: Mon. Admission charge.

Muro is 42km northeast of Palma, 13km east of Inca. Tourist Office: Avda. Albufera, 33. Tel: (971) 89 10 13.

Petra
Most visitors to this remote inland town are American, for Petra is the birthplace of Junípero Serra (1713–84), founder of the Spanish Missions that grew into the State of California (*see pp40–41*). With its tall old buildings and a maze of narrow streets, the town seems hardly to have changed since his day. Fortunately, there are signs directing you to the sights associated with its famous son, who was beatified in 1988.

At the eastern end of the town is the parish church of Sant Pere, which has a lovely large, stained-glass rose window. For an overview of the area, visit the nearby Ermita de Bonany (*see p111*).

Museu y Casa Natal Fray Junípero Serra
Small but well laid out, the museum brings home the epic achievements of the Franciscan friar who left the island for Mexico in 1749. Beautifully made wooden models show the missions he founded in California, growing ever larger and more ornate over the years. Nine were established between San Diego and San Francisco during 1769–82, and another 12 after his death.

In the same street is the simple house where Serra was born, with a tiny loft-like bedroom and a minute garden at the rear. Across from the entrance, a short lane leads to the **Convent de Sant Bernadó**, a mighty 17th-century church with a monument to the friar outside. Painted tiles framed with wrought iron depict the missions Serra founded – a gift from the people of California.
Carrer Barracar Alt 6–8. Tel: (971) 56 11 49. Visitors by appointment only.

Petra is 50km east of Palma, 10km northwest of Manacor.

Climb the steps of Pollença's Calvari for salvation and magnificent views

PROBLEM IN
POLLENÇA

The Badia de Pollença is the setting for a short story by English crime writer Agatha Christie. *Problem at Pollensa Bay* describes the elaborate strategy of a son to break free from his over-protective mother and find love with a modern girl. Ending with a characteristic twist to the plot, the tale evokes a pre-war world when well-spoken English holidaymakers with 'excellent hotel manners' (as Christie describes them) came to Mallorca on the steamer from Barcelona. They would take a taxi to the new hotels around Port de Pollença, then relax with games of piquet and cocktails on the terrace.

Pollença

Reached by a fast road from Palma (C713), Pollença rests in foothills at the eastern end of the Serra de Tramuntana. This attractive town is a haven of sleepy Mallorcan traditions, where café life and the siesta roll on as if package holidaymakers had never been invented. The somewhat austere buildings lining the dusty streets, with their ochre roofs, sun-baked walls, and faded wooden shutters, could be virtually anywhere in Spain – as could the street-choking traffic. Do not be deterred by Pollença's parking problems. Leave your vehicle in one of the car parks on the south side of town and walk in to the Plaça Major.

Pollença was put on the map by the Romans, and a Pont Romá still spans the Torrente de Sant Jordi River to the north of the town (just off the C710 to Lluc). After the Spanish conquest of

Ostriches regularly inspect vehicles touring the Auto Safari

beaches are narrow and divided by breakwaters, with shallow water well suited to young children.

Go to the southern end of the bay for watersports, as well as tennis, riding and bowling. In the back streets and squares behind the seafront there is a range of 'pick-a-fish' restaurants and others serving *tipico* Mallorcan cuisine.

Port de Pollença has a relaxed, distinguished air with no nightclubs or blaring discos, though you will find plenty of music and entertainment in restaurants and hotels. The admirable Spanish institution known as the evening *paseo* (promenade) thrives here, with plenty of recruits from the resort's sizeable community of foreign residents and retired visitors taking a long winter break. For the elderly or people with disabilities, Port de Pollença is one of the most congenial destinations on the island.
57km northeast of Palma, 6km northeast of Pollença. Tourist Office: Calle Monges. Tel: (971) 86 54 67.

Excursions in the Bay

The Port de Pollença area is the centre for sightseeing excursions and glass-bottomed boats to beaches and sights around the bay. Glass-bottomed boats make excursions around the bay to see the shoreline and the undersea life, Monday–Friday 3–5.30pm, and return trips to Formentor Point, at the tip of the peninsula, Monday–Wednesday, Friday 10.30am–1pm. A ferry takes passengers to Formentor Beach, daily on the hour 10am–3pm, returning on the half hour. On Thursdays, a catamaran travels to Cala San Vicente for one return trip, 10.30am–2pm. A quiet resort with three separate bays, Cala San Vincente is home to the Caves of l'Alzinaret. This ancient burial site is at the edge of the resort area, in Los Encinares park.
Boats, tel: (971) 86 40 14. Purchase tickets opposite the Brisa Marina.

S'Albufera
See p140.

Sheep grazing near Sa Colònia de Sant Pere

Sa Colònia de Sant Pere

At the southern end of Badia d'Alcúdia, this quiet fishing village is slowly developing into a resort. Behind it rises Puig den Ferrutx and the mountains of the Serra d'Artà, with the nearby countryside rich with vines, almond and apricot trees, and olive groves decorated with fat, woolly sheep. There is a tiny harbour, a beach that is part rock, part sand, a Club Nautico, a few shops and simple fish restaurants.

The campsite at the western end of the village makes a quiet base for budget travellers, with good walks around Ermita de Betlem (*see p138*) and Puig de Morei.

83km east of Palma, 13km northwest of Artà. Take the C712 from Artà or Can Picafort and turn north (PM333-1), forking left after 5km for the village.

Ses Païsses

The ruins of this Bronze Age settlement are an evocative legacy of the inhabitants of Mallorca between 1000–800 BC. The impressive portal and most of the perimeter walls are still in place. Some of the blocks used to build this settlement weigh up to eight tonnes.

The site was probably occupied during Roman times. It is not difficult to picture the halls and dwellings, and the lookout tower that would have warned of approaching ships.

Today, Ses Païsses is surrounded by fields covered with almond and carob trees, and the area makes a pleasant picnic spot.

68km east of Palma, 2km south of Artà. Turn left off the C715 to Capdepera, down a signposted track. Admission charge.

you can sometimes see Cabrera island. *37km southeast of Palma. Take the road from S'Arenal to Cap Blanc, or from Llucmajor towards Cala Pi, then follow signs to the site. Tel: (971) 18 01 55. Open: Fri–Wed 10am–5pm. Closed: Thur. Admission charge. Access may be difficult for visitors with disabilities.*

Castell de Santueri

Castell de Santueri is strategically sited at the summit of a 408-m peak in the Serra de Llevant. Protected by steep cliffs, it was rebuilt in the 14th century above the ruins of a Moorish stronghold. Only parts of the outer walls and ramparts remain. Walking around the vast interior can become a scramble (unsuitable for small children), but the wildflowers and views make it worthwhile.

57km southeast of Palma, 6.5km southeast of Felanitx. Take the road for Santanyí, turning left after 2km on to a country road that runs through fields and orchards, then climbs up to the castle. Open: daily 10am–7pm. Admission charge.

Coves del Drac

The Coves del Drac (Dragon Caves) were first explored in 1896 by a French geologist, Édouard Martel, and now attract thousands of visitors every year. The entrance to the caves is down a steep flight of steps, followed by a walk along narrow, but well-lit, underground passages and platforms (not for the claustrophobic).

The labyrinth of tunnels and caves is estimated to run for about 2km in total, and fanciful names have been given to many of its physical features. Visitors are guided to the delights of Diana's Bath and the Fairies' Theatre, passing through a fairyland of radiant pools, and stalactites and stalagmites dramatically illuminated by concealed lights in various colours. The tour culminates in the vast Lago Martel and a cavernous auditorium that can hold over a thousand spectators. The show features a torchlight procession with musicians and singers gliding across the water in boats.

66km east of Palma, 1.5km south of Porto Cristo. Tel: (971) 82 07 53. Open: daily, Apr–Oct with tours on the hour from 10am to 5pm; during the rest of the year 10.45am–noon, 2.30pm & 4.30pm. Admission charge.

An attractive sign welcomes visitors inside the Dragon Caves

Caves

The caves that formed naturally in Mallorca's limestone rocks have always been useful to its islanders. They provided shelter for the Pre-Talayot settlers (*see pp10–11*) who set up home here around 2000 BC, and are a common thread through the island's social history. Caves served as dank homes for mythical beasts, provided refuge from slave-raiders and lairs for pirates, and were used as smugglers' dens as well as religious sanctuaries. Rediscovered in the late 19th century, the largest and strangest are now technicolour tourist attractions for hordes of sightseers.

Marine caves are created by the quarrying action of the waves. Inland, caves are created as water containing carbon dioxide circulates through the joints and faults in the calcareous rock. In time, the passages and channels formed become caverns which are revealed when the water table drops. This process can create extraordinary deposits, including stalagmites (spikes rising from the ground), stalactites (like icicles hanging from above), draperies (like curtains), and knobbly clusters known as cave coral.

The caves at Artà (*see p99*), probably the best on the island, are said to have inspired Jules Verne's book, *Journey to the Centre of the Earth*. The phantasmagoric rock shapes continue to stimulate the imagination. Once likened to pious subjects such as the Virgin, a cathedral, or grottoes fit for classical deities, these drip-fed rock blobs are now more often seen to resemble human towers, monstrous hairy nostrils, the Leaning Tower of Pisa, eggs and bacon, or vegetables in a great subterranean *supermercado*.

Caves (*coves*) can be visited at Drac (*p121*), Hams (*p124*), Artà (*p99*), Campanet (*p71*) and Gènova (*pp54–5*). Since the temperature inside is constant all year round (about 20°C/68°F), you do not need a coat, but as the ground can be wet and slippery, wear suitable shoes.

Facing page: awesome formations of stalagmites and stalactites inside a cave;
above: the gaping entrance at Artà

Coves dels Hams

The Coves dels Hams get their name from the similarity of stalactites hanging in some caves to *hams*, a Mallorcan word for fish-hooks. Though the caves are not as extensive as the nearby Coves del Drac (*see p121*), their underground formations, which were only discovered in 1906, are an impressive natural sight, made easily accessible by guided tour. Highlights include the 'Lake of Venice' and rock formations that resemble everything from saints and petrified cities to a herd of elephants. Coloured lights and a *concierto* (concert) enhance the occasion.

60km east of Palma, 2km west of Porto Cristo. Tel: (971) 82 09 88. Open: daily, Apr–Oct 10am–6pm; Nov–Mar 10.30am–5pm. Admission charge.

Ermita de Sant Salvador

A physical and spiritual high point of the island, the Ermita de Sant Salvador is approached by a convoluted series of bends that climb up Puig de Sant Salvador (509m), the summit of the Serra de Llevant. During the ascent you pass a small chapel, the 12 Stations of the Cross, a large stone cross and a 37-m high statue of Christ the King.

A well with ladle greets thirsty visitors to the monastery. Inside the huge gatehouse is a Gothic depiction of the Last Supper and offerings left by pilgrims that include pictures of local cyclists and their jerseys. The 18th-century church has a Bethlehem Grotto (a Nativity scene viewed through magnifying windows), and a revered Virgin.

As photographs, crutches, toys and

The church of Sant Miquel, Felanitx: Baroque flourishes on a plain canvas

notes left in the small room by the entrance testify, the Ermita continues to represent a crucial source of spiritual aid. There is a simple restaurant.

57km southeast of Palma, 4km southeast of Felanitx. Take the road to Porto Colom, turning right after 2km on to a country road.

Felanitx

Felanitx is a traditional market town on the west flank of the Serra de Llevant. Its name is thought to be derived, rather poetically, from *fiel a nit* ('faithful to the night'). Seven roads converge on the town, which can make parking in the narrow streets leading to its market square something of an endurance test.

The square is dominated by the 13th-century church of Sant Miquel, a large, warm-stoned edifice with broad steps leading up to the Renaissance doorway. The Baroque façade includes a memorial plaque to 414 victims killed when a wall in the town collapsed in 1844.

shrubs and flowers, such as French lavender, rosemary, heather and the colourful strawberry tree (*Arbutus unedo*). The route crosses several other tracks, then skirts eastward round a hill, Puig de Sa Comuna. As you start to climb, a huge stone statue of Christ will soon come into view.
Continue up a narrow track, which rises to a small ridge.

Ermita (Santuari) de Sant Salvador

From here you can see the great buildings of the Ermita de Sant Salvador. The route now follows a well-worn path that rises steeply. The effort of the climb will be admirably rewarded by the splendid view from the *ermita*, where water, food and an antiquated toilet await the walker. Founded in the 14th century, this magnificent sanctuary has become a magnet for both tourists and religious pilgrims (*see p124*). The Santuari can also be reached by leaving Felanitx in the direction of Portocolom, a 2km path to Sant Salvador, a stiff climb but easy and well marked; no right-of-way problems.

Retrace your steps to return to your starting point.

Trees of Gold
The carob tree (*Ceratonia siliqua*), sometimes known as the locust tree, thrives in the hot arid soil of the Mediterranean region. The tree has thick shiny leaves, a gnarled trunk and long seedpods that turn from green to black as they ripen. High in sugar, these are primarily used as animal feed. The fruit of the carob is also made into a chocolate substitute sold in health food stores. The word 'carat', used today as a unit of weight for gold and precious stones, derives from the word carob. The Arabs knew the fruit as *kirat*, and the Greeks as *keration*.

The Ermita de Sant Salvador was built on the summit of the Serra de Llevant

On your bike: cyclists coasting along the level seafront at Port de Pollença

Getting Away From It All

The clichéd view of Mallorca as two islands – one passionately devoted to summer holiday fun, and the other real, rural and eternal – is perfectly true. A visit to Mallorca is not complete until you have sneaked off to at least one of its quieter corners. No matter where you stay, all parts of the island are accessible in a day trip.

BOAT TRIPS

Taking to the sea is a good way to escape the crowds, and at the same time see Mallorca from a different viewpoint. You can observe underwater marine life from aboard a glass-bottomed boat. Some trips call into beaches, coves and sea-caves that would otherwise be impossible to reach – notably the 100-m long **Cova Blava** (Blue Cave) on the island of Cabrera, where the reflection of light creates an intense blue.

Except in the Badia de Palma, excursions run only in the summer (May to October, in many cases) and often take the best part of a day: check if you need to bring a packed lunch, and put on plenty of suntan cream. Tourist offices and resorts have a detailed leaflet of excursion times and prices. (Signs saying *alrededores* mean a short trip in the waters close to your departure point.)

Nearly every town along the coast has sightseeing boats of some variety, from glass-bottomed so you can see the well-protected marine life around the island, to conventional boats from which you can admire the sea cliffs and bird life.

Cabrera

The archipelago of Cabrera, a group of islands off the southern tip of Mallorca, also a natural park (*see pp140–41*), can be reached by boat from the ports of Colònia de Sant Jordi and Portopetra. Both are all-day trips, the first heading for Cabrera and the second to the neighbouring island of Cruceros Llevant. Passengers can book with or without the option of lunch. *Tel: (971) 64 90 34 (Cabrera) or (971) 65 70 12 (Cruceros Llevant).*

Sa Dragonera

Excursion boats cross the Es Freu channel that separates Mallorca and the island of Sa Dragonera (*see p140*), leaving from Sant Elm and Port d'Andratx. The quickest is the 20-minute crossing from Sant Elm aboard *Margarita*, which operates regularly throughout the day. For bookings *tel: (639) 61 75 45 or (696) 42 39 33.*

CYCLING

Cycling in Mallorca is a growth industry. The Spanish take it very seriously, and every Sunday the hills appear alive with luridly coloured insects covering great distances and heights with astonishing ease. It is usually too hot in July and August to enjoy a major expedition, but you can have a good time just by hiring a bike in a resort for a day and pottering along the coast. Some hotels have bicycles for rent, or there are specialist shops. Family bicycles with seats for two adults and four children are sometimes available; you may be asked for a deposit. (Bicycles can be hired from Can Pashlla, *tel: (971) 49 03 58.*)

The Badia d'Alcúdia is obligingly flat, and a cycle path runs between Port d'Alcúdia and Can Picafort. You can also cycle in the S'Albufera nature reserve. Another *pista de bicicletas* (cycle track) curls round the centre of the Badia de Palma from Portixol west to Sa Pedrera, passing right along Palma's seafront; Castell de Bellver makes a rewarding goal. Many other areas are also introducing cycle paths.

If you prefer more of a challenge, ask for the *Guia del Ciclista* map, available from tourist offices. This details six itineraries ranging from 70km to 150km, including a masochistic 14-km ascent from Sa Calobra.

HIDDEN CORNERS

There is nowhere on Mallorca that is 'undiscovered', but it is not hard to find somewhere that feels well away from it all. The following destinations all offer a degree of escape.

Cap Blanc

A breezy headland at the southwest corner of the island with white cliffs dropping sheer to the sea 60m below. The cliff-edges are unguarded, but you can follow an invigorating walk that leads west from the lighthouse.

Cala Mesquida

In the northeast corner of the island, a once-secluded beach reached by a 8-km road north from Capdepera. Though busy in summer, it can be pleasantly quiet out of season.

Cala Sant Vicenç
See p97.

Castell d'Alaró
See p70.

Cap de Ses Salines

The flat, southern tip of the island offers views across the sea to Cabrera. Military land restricts walking.

Boat trippers leaving Port de Pollença

5·PM·16·92

Ermita de Betlem

A remote mountain sanctuary (380m) reached by a tortuous road that winds for 10km northwest of Artà. Founded in 1805, Ermita de Betlem is still home to hermits, who no doubt find spiritual succour in the stupendous views.

Galilea

See p56.

Orient

See p77.

Puigpunyent

See p62.

Punta de n'Amer

A respite from the resorts on the east coast, Punta de n'Amer can be reached by walking north from Sa Coma or south from Cala Millor. The 17th-century Castell de n'Amer has a deep moat and ramparts, offers fine coastal views, and is the high point of this 200-hectare protected headland. It was here that Republican forces from Menorca landed during the Spanish Civil War.

LA RESERVA

On the eastern slopes of Puig de Galatzó (1,026m), this privately-owned nature reserve is an easy introduction to the countryside of Mallorca's Serra de Tramuntana. A network of steps and purpose-built paths will lead you through a 20,000-hectare park which has dense woods, 30 waterfalls, springs, caves and rocky limestone outcrops. Wooden plaques provide information along the way about La Reserva's numerous plants: most grow naturally, while the rest have been introduced from around the island.

La Reserva took seven years to be completed – and it shows. There are handrails beside steep steps, plenty of strategically placed benches to regain your breath, and information boards in several languages giving a background on subjects such as unusual rock formations and birdlife. Additional points of interest include a charcoal burner's hut, a 1,000-year-old olive tree and the **Cova des Moro** (Cave of the Moor, Point 9).

The walk takes 90 minutes. If you are going by car, try not to arrive too late – so that you can avoid having to drive your vehicle back down the mountains in the dark. On Fridays in the summer, you can also visit the park on a coach excursion from Santa Ponça and Peguera.

18km west of Palma, 4km west of Puigpunyent, signposted on the Puigpunyent-Galilea road.
Tel: (971) 61 66 22. Open: daily, winter 10am–6.30pm; summer 10am–7pm.
Last admission: 2 hours before closing time. Closed: Mon–Tue. Admission charge.

Charcoal Burners

Among the ancient mule tracks and goat-trodden paths that criss-cross the Mallorcan countryside are routes forged by the island's *carbonero*s (charcoal burners). Until the arrival of the gas bottle in the 1920s, Mallorcans used charcoal as fuel. The burners and their families would move into the forests for the summer, building temporary homes and circular mounds of stones where the charcoal was made. Vast quantities of wood needed to be gathered using only axes and saws, and the fires had to be constantly tended. Walkers will encounter abandoned moss-covered *sitjas* (charcoal ovens) – forlorn monuments to an arduous trade.

Another Mallorca: the S'Albufera wetlands are an unexpected treat for nature-lovers

10 22. Open: daily, winter 9am–4pm; summer 9am–1pm & 2–5pm. Free admission.

S'ALBUFERA

The name derives from the Arabic *al-Buhayra*, meaning 'small lake.' First mentioned in Roman times, the marshes were later used as hunting grounds, and in the 17th century, divided into self-irrigating cultivable plots. From the early 20th century to the 1960s, when the northern end was sold off for tourist development, the area was used to grow rice. In 1985, 800 hectares were bought by the Balearic Islands government for conservation.

Pay a visit to the Parc Natural de S'Albufera today and you will encounter a wholly unexpected aspect of Mallorca. Marked paths, some of which can be cycled, guide visitors around the level marshland – a hushed world of bridges, hides and observation points tucked away among the lakes, reed beds and grassy undergrowth.

Birds are the main attraction – more than 200 species have so far been recorded, including ospreys, falcons and numerous marsh birds. Frogs, snakes, insects and colourful wildflowers such as the grape hyacinth and elegant orchids add to the natural show.

5km south of Port d'Alcúdia. Turn west by the Pont dels Anglesos on the Alcúdia-Artà road. Tel: (971) 89 22 50. Open: daily, summer 9am–6pm; winter 9am–5pm. By donation.

PARC NATURAL DE MONDRAGÓ

Designated as a conservation area, the park offers a rich flora and fauna amid attractive landscapes of pines, shrubs, small lakes and dunes. The area also borders the sea, and has two of the most attractive coves to be found along Mallorca's eastern coast. Examples of traditional architecture can also be seen.

Major points of interest, linked by pathways, are the Ca Na Martina, Niu de Metralladores, Ca Na Muda and Aula de Mar, where aquariums display local sea life. An information office gives advice on the area.

4–9km east/northeast of Santanyí. For the easiest route take the road northeast to S'Alqueria Blanca. Entry point is to the right, 8km from Santanyí. Tel: (971) 18

SA DRAGONERA

The dramatic island of Sa Dragonera

provides a spectacular focus for boat excursions from Sant Telm and Port d'Andratx. A steep, bare wedge of rock rising to 353m, it can be explored on foot via walking trails to the summit of Puig de sa Pòpia, to the Tramuntana lighthouse (at the northeast tip) and the Llebeig lighthouse, to the southeast. Walking times vary from 30 to 90 minutes and all trails are well signposted from the little museum and visitors centre at Cala Lladó, the arrival point for boats. At Cova de sa Font are Roman remains. (*For boat excursions, see p136.*)

WALKING

With its absorbing variety of mountain, coast and plain, along with countless sanctuaries, watchtowers and castles to provide rewarding goals, Mallorca is ideal for walkers. Good launch pads, with generally quiet accommodation, are Banyalbufar, Port d'Andratx, Port de Sóller and Port de Pollença. There is a good case for staying in or near Palma, as it is the focal point for all bus routes.

Several specialist books on walking in Mallorca are available. Try to buy them before you leave home. Some local tourist offices, notably those in the Calvià area, produce free booklets with suggested routes.

The Serra de Tramuntana, with its cool forests and wide-ranging views, is the most appealing area for walking. The island's good bus service means that in many cases you do not need to hire a car – Sóller and Lluc are popular starting points. Caution is always required: beware the fierce heat and sun in summer, and mists and wet ground at other times of the year.

CABRERA

Cabrera (or Goat) island lies 18km off Mallorca's south coast – and at roughly 7km by 5km it is the largest among all the scattered islets. Cabrera's coastline is indented and craggy, rising no higher than Na Picamosques (171m), the 'Fly Bite'. In 1991, Cabrera became a protected Parque Nacional Marítimo Terrestre (National Land-Sea Park), the first of its kind in Spain, and a symbol of the triumph of ecological lobbying.

Today, the island is virtually uninhabited, but its rocks are forever stained by a grim episode during the Peninsular War when 9,000 French prisoners of war were dumped here following the Spanish victory at Bailén in 1808. Left with only meagre water and rations, the defeated soldiers fell victim to disease, indiscipline and chronic thirst. By 1814, when the survivors were finally taken off, more than 5,000 prisoners had died. A monument near the small port remembers the victims of this tragedy. In 1916 Cabrera was taken over for military use, and a handful of soldiers are still stationed on the island – now joined by visiting scientists, naturalists and day trippers from the mainland.

Cabrera has a superb natural harbour, and the island was often used as a stepping-stone for pirates raiding the Balearic Islands. The shell of a 14th-century castle-cum-prison still stands on a nearby hill top, but is officially out of bounds.

The appeal of Cabrera today is its rarity: a wilderness island in the midst of the over-developed Mediterranean. Among the many birds attracted to the island are Eleonora's falcons, cormorants and a colony of rare Audouin's gulls. Wild goats, an exclusive sub-species of Lilford's wall lizard, and a rich marine life all thrive here. *Boat excursions to Cabrera depart*

from the port at Sa Colònia de Sant Jordi daily from May to mid-Oct. Tel: (971) 64 90 34. The boat leaves at 9.30am and returns at 5.30pm – take a picnic, swimming costume and snorkel. Information on the island is available from the Sa Colònia de Sant Jordi tourist office, see p130.

The rugged coast makes for a great day out on a boat

Shopping

Palma is the place to shop in Mallorca. Specialist factories making glass, artificial pearls, leather goods and carved olive-wood items are also worth visiting. Their wares are not necessarily cheaper than in normal shops, but it is always fun to know the provenance of your purchases.

Many Mallorcan souvenirs are handmade

Opening Times

Shops generally open up between 9am and 10am depending on what they deal in – those selling fresh produce open earliest. By 1.30pm they are closing down for lunch. They re-open around 4.30–5.30pm, then remain open until 8pm. Shops tend to have longer opening hours in the summer, and in the resorts some stay open through the lunch

Traditional flamenco dress for sale in Pollença

break, as do hypermarkets. Department stores and fashion shops in Palma also stay open during the siesta. On Saturday, shops are open only in the morning. For the truly indefatigable shopper, the great department store El Corte Inglés has two branches in Palma, at Avinguda Alejandre Roselló 1216a and Avinguda Jaume III 15. These are open Monday to Saturday from 10am to 9–10pm. English is spoken in many shops.

Spain is a procrastinator's paradise, and the spirit of *mañana* ('Why do today what can be put off till the morrow?') thrives in a happy-go-lucky island like Mallorca. In some country shops it can take so long to be served it might be necessary to check the sell-by date on your purchases.

Prices

Shoes, T-shirts and casual clothing are good value, and '60 centimo' shops, where all goods are theoretically that price or less, is a purse-friendly way to indulge the children. Many shops appear to be in a permanent state of sale (*rebaja*). Sizes of clothes and shoes will be in metric and European sizes (*see p179* for conversion tables). Bartering is rarely necessary, though the itinerant market vendors from West Africa found

Palma has the best choice of shops, with a web of traffic-free streets to explore

in markets and seafront pitches will oblige. It is a common diversion at Palma's Rastrillo flea market.

Souvenirs

The range of items for sale bearing the word 'Mallorca' or a relevant image is a tribute to the ingenuity of the islanders. While some goods are mesmerisingly unnecessary to world progress, glass, kitchen pottery, olive-wood utensils, candlesticks, tableware, tea towels and beachwear are worth considering. A comprehensive range of Spanish and Mallorcan souvenirs can be found at the Poble Espanyol complex in Palma (*see p45*). Local craftmaking skills are also displayed here.

Supermarkets

All the resorts have well-stocked supermarkets. Years of experience have taught owners about the money to be made from selling tomato ketchup, Heinz beans and Marmite, and there is little need to take such staples out to Mallorca. Imported goods tend to cost more than Spanish brands. Vegetables are sold by the kilo, and at fish, meat or delicatessen counters remember that you usually have to take a numbered ticket from a machine to be served in turn.

If you are staying in a self-catering apartment or inland villa, it may help to load up your rented car at one of the hypermarkets on the outskirts of Palma. You need a €1 coin to get a trolley; in some premises, any other shopping must be sealed in a bag before entering. Hypermarkets are generally open from 10am to 10pm, Monday to Saturday (*see pp146–8 for shops*).

Island Crafts

'The first difficulty that a stranger encounters on a shopping expedition in a Majorcan village is the absence not only of shop signs but of shop fronts. Everybody knows where the shopkeeper lives, so why should he announce it?'

GORDON WEST

Jogging Round Mallorca 1929

It is ironic that the best souvenirs Mallorca produces are also the most breakable. Among the glut of holiday merchandise on sale around the island, the brittle, curious *siurell* is the one craft product that feels truly Mallorcan. Made from clay and often painted white with flashes of red and green, these ancient tokens of friendship usually take the shape of a figure on a donkey in a hat or playing a guitar. The origin of the *siurell* is uncertain. They are known to have existed in Moorish times but probably date from much earlier. Artist Joan Miró was fond of these naïve works, which are mostly made around Marratxí. They come in varying sizes and incorporate a crude whistle at the base.

Glass is another exceptional product and has been made on the island since Roman times. In the 16th century, Mallorcan glassware rivalled that of Venice, and today's bestselling products often reproduce historic designs. Since the 1960s the island has had three glassmaking centres – the best known is

Handmade: attractive semi-glazed brown pottery made in Felanitx (facing page); carved olive wood (left); pottery student at Poble Espanyol, Palma (below)

Casa Gordiola at Algaida. Here visitors can see craftsmen hand-blowing the glass, which is made in dark green, cobalt and amber hues. Jugs, drinking glasses, vases and candle-holders are popular buys.

A robust, semi-glazed brown pottery is made in Felanitx, and the Sunday morning market here is a good place to pick up cooking bowls or jugs.

Local olive wood is carved into domestic utensils and ornaments at the Oliv-Art factory near Manacor; the mellow-grained wood is hard-wearing and makes worthwhile presents.

Roba de llengues, literally cloth of tongues, are a striking feature of the Mallorcan home. Made mainly in Pollença and Santa Marie del Cami, this durable and reversible cotton material often comes in zigzagging red, green or blue patterns and is used for curtains, bedspreads, wall furnishings and upholstery.

Where to Buy
IN PALMA

All the useful shops are within the boundary of the city's old walls. Most of them are to the east of Passeig des Born where many streets are traffic-free. Whether you actually have things to buy or just enjoy the bustle of a city at play, the streets and squares listed below are all worth getting to know. The most enjoyable time for exploration is early evening, when the Palmese go window-shopping, how-do-you-do-ing and buying cakes – all traditions of the Spanish *paseo* (promenade).

Avinguda Jaume III: Palma's quality shopping street.
Carrer de Sindicat: bargain clothes, shoes, spices.
Carrer de Sant Miquel: links Plaça Major and the market.
Carrer de Platería: jewellery shops galore.
Carrer de Jaume II: fans, umbrellas, boutiques.
Plaça Major: Revamped underground shopping centre with leather clothing, handbags and shoes. Souvenirs and supermarket.

La Rambla: flower stalls and newspaper kiosks.
Porto Pi: Shopping centre on two floors with branches of well-known Palma fashion shops, ethnic shops, home accessories and handmade chocolates.

Antiques
Linares
Close to the cathedral, it sells good value items.
Plaça Almoina 4.
Tel: (971) 71 72 19.
Midge Dalton
Antique jewellery and small articles. Mostly silver.
Placa Mercat, 20.
Tel: (971) 71 33 60.
Persepolis
High-class antiques in main shopping street.
Avinguda de Jaume III.
Tel: (971) 72 45 39.

Books
The Bookworm
Paseo del Mar, 32.
Tel: (971) 68 23 25.

Cakes and Chocolates
Frasquet
Chocolates and sweets for all moods.
Carrer Orfila, 4.
Tel: (971) 72 13 54.
Forn d'es Teatre
Most photographed cake shop in Palma.

A shrine to *sobrasada* (spiced sausage) at Carrer de Santo Domingo, Palma

Plaça Weyler 11.
Tel: (971) 71 52 54.
Forn Fondo
The place for *ensaimadas*.
Carrer de l'Unió 15.
Tel: (971) 71 16 34.

Crafts
Artesanías
Ceramics, china, glass.
Carrer de l'Unió 13.
Tel: (971) 72 42 99.
Alpargatería Llinás
Straw-woven goods.
Carrer de Sant Miquel 43.
Tel: (971) 71 76 96.
Cesteria del Centro
Straw-woven baskets and other articles.
Carrer d'en Brossa, 6.
Tel: (971) 72 45 33.
Ninot Tauro
Unusual ornaments and sculptures. Paintings.

Plaça La Llotja.
Tel: (971) 72 35 24.

Food and Drink
Colmado Santo
Domingo
Abundance of Mallorcan
delicacies.
Carrer de Sant Domingo 5.
La Montaña
Cheeses and sausages of
all kinds.
Carrer de Jaume II 29.
Tel: (971) 71 25 95.

Glass
Gordiola
Vidrio soplado (hand-
blown glass).
Carrer de Victoria 2.
Tel: (971) 71 15 41.

Home Accessories
Bellacasa Inmobilaria
Towels, bed and table linen.
Plaça Cort 13.
Tel: (971) 71 61 00.
Casa Bet Merceria
Cotton, lace, belts,
tapestries.
Carrer de Bosseria 6.
Tel: (971) 72 20 69.
Herederos de Vicente
Juan
Different locations. There
is a wide variety at:
Carrer de Sant Nicolau 10.
Tel: (971) 72 17 73.
Josefa Segura
Hand-embroidered
articles and household
linen.

Pescateria Vella, 5.
Tel: (971) 71 67 03.
Nobile
Kilims and oriental rugs.
San Miquel, 75.
Tel: (971) 71 30 98.
Textiles Personalizadas
Your own designs copied
in hand or machine
embroidery.
Calle Colom, 16.
Tel: (971) 71 69 55.

Hypermarkets
Carre Four
Avinguda Cardenal
Rossell, Coll Rebassa.
Tel: (971) 26 67 00.
Carre Four
Avinguda General Riera
156–72.
Tel: (971) 76 63 00.

Pearls and Jewellery
Carrer d'Argenteria
and **Carrer de Plateria**
are full of jewellery
shops.
Perlas Orquídea
Artificial pearls.
Plaça Rei Joan Carles I.
Tel: (971) 71 57 97.

Porcelain
Souvenir shops can be
found by the score.
Maria Begoña Merino
Lladró porcelain and
other fine china.
La Rambla dels Ducs de
Palma de Mallorca, 15.
Tel: (971) 72 14 09.

Nacar
Lladró porcelain and
other fine china.
Avda, Jaume III, 5.
Tel: (971) 71 58 48.

Stamps and Coins
Pampa
Carrer de Conquistador 3.
Tel: (971) 72 33 82.
Filatelia Mallorca
Caputxins, 7 bajo.
Tel: (971) 71 14 18.

AROUND THE ISLAND
Antiques
Antiguedades Gaul
Avinguda de Rei Jaume II,
No. 153, Inca.
Tel: (971) 50 28 48.
Galeria Rustic
Bernat de Santa Eugènia,
78, Santa Maria del Cami.
Tel: (971) 62 07 31.

Ceramics
Artesania Goddy
Carrer Carmen, 37,
Port de Pollença.
Tel: (971) 86 43 43.
Ceramicas C'an Bernat
Traditional Mallorcan
pottery articles.
Bartolomeu Pascual, s/n,
Santa Maria del Cami.
Tel: (971) 62 13 06.

Glass
Casa Gordiola
Hand-blown glass.
Carretera Manacor, km19,
Algaida. Tel: (971) 66 50 46.

Lafiore
Carretera Vella de
Valldemossa, km1.
Tel: (971) 61 01 40.

Household Accessories

Henriettas
Household accessories,
mirrors, lamps and
glassware.
Ctra. França, 2, S'Arraco.
Tel: (971) 67 29 16;
henriettas@ocea.es

Leather Goods

Inca is the centre of
Mallorca's leather
industry and there is a
very wide choice.

Olive Wood Articles

Artesania Olivo
Bernat Fiol
Carrer Bon Jesús 10,
Consell.
Tel: (971) 62 21 58.
Artesanía Madera
Roselló
Jordi Sureda, 69, Manacor.
Tel: (971) 55 32 89.

Pearls and Jewellery

L'Or de Mallorca
Carrer de Blanquerna 10,
Valldemossa.
Tel: (971) 61 61 14.
Perlas Orquídea
Carretera Palma–Manacor
km 30, Montuïri.
Tel: (971) 64 41 44.
www.perlasorquidea.com

Supermarkets
Caprabo
Chain of giant stores.
Avinguda Bienvenidos,
Cala d'Or,
tel: (971) 65 80 24;
Avinguda de las
Palmeres, Sa Coma,
tel: (971) 81 08 35;
Avinguda Jaume I,
Santa Ponça, tel: (971) 69
29 50; and others.

Markets

Mallorca's markets are
worth visiting for their
local character as much
as for the articles on
sale. Local fruit is well
worth buying, and you
may see some pottery
or leather goods that
appeal. Beware
pickpockets and
importuning ladies
selling flowers and
tablecloths.

Of the regular weekly
markets listed below, the
most worth seeking out
are the daily produce
market in Palma's Plaça
de l'Olivar, the
traditional Wednesday
livestock-and-everything
jamboree in Sineu, and
the sprawling Thursday
morning market in Inca.
Unless otherwise stated,
all are morning markets
(and are usually fading
fast by 1pm).

PALMA
Plaça del Olivar
This is a good place to
buy the best of local and
imported produce as
well as specialities like
sobrasada and cheese
from Menorca. In
addition to fruit and
vegetables there is a
meat hall upstairs, a
fish hall to the side,
several *tapas* bars and
even a small public
library.
Mon–Sat 8.30am–1pm.

Rastrillo
(Flea Market)
Junk, secondhand
household goods, reject
china, lurid plastic toys
and the odd antique.
Expect to barter for your
bargains.
Lower part of Avinguda
GA Villalonga.
Open: Sat morning
8am–2pm.

Plaça Major
A number of crafts stalls
selling a variety of
jewellery, souvenirs,
folk art.
Mon, Fri & Sat
10am–2pm.

Market Days

WEST OF PALMA
Andratx Wednesday
Calvià Monday

NORTHWEST

Alaró Saturday
Binissalem Friday
Bunyola Saturday
Campanet Tuesday
Consell Sunday Flea
market
Pont d'Inca Friday
Santa Eugènia Saturday
Santa Maria Sunday
Sencelles Wednesday
Sóller Saturday
Valldemossa Sunday

NORTHEAST

Alcúdia Tuesday and
Sunday
Artà Tuesday
Cala Rajada Saturday
Can Picafort Friday
Capdepera Wednesday

Costitx Saturday
Inca Thursday and
Sunday
Lloseta Saturday
Llubí Tuesday
Maria de la Salut Friday
Montuïri Monday
Muro Sunday
Pollença Sunday
Port de Pollença
Wednesday
Sa Pobla Sunday
**Sant Llorenç des
Cardassar** Thursday
Santa Margalida
Tuesday & Saturday
Selva Wednesday
Sineu Wednesday
Son Servera Friday
Vilafranca de Bonany
Wednesday

SOUTH

Algaida Thursday
Campos Thursday and
Saturday
Can Pastilla Tuesday and
Thursday
Felanitx Sunday
Llucmajor Wednesday
Manacor Monday and
Saturday
Porreres Tuesday
Porto Colom Tuesday
and Saturday
Porto Cristo Sunday
S'Arenal Thursday
Sa Colònia de Sant Jordi
Wednesday
Santanyí Wednesday
and Saturday
Ses Salines Thursday

Stall selling table linen in Palma's Rastrillo, a flea market held every Saturday

Entertainment

In the resorts, the music, shows and nightlife are geared to the international tastes of the briefly visiting holidaymaker. Alongside this popular entertainment, the Mallorcans have their own cultural activities, including a busy calendar of religious and secular celebrations.

British pubs, German bars: there's no shortage of watering-holes in the resorts

Where to Go

What's On, a free quarterly in English with an up-to-date listing of sporting and cultural activities in the Balearic Islands, is available from tourist offices. Programmes and topical events are also advertised in local papers and tourist-orientated publications (*see p180*).

Bear in mind that the Spanish like to party late, and local *festes* may not really get going till well after the times advertised. In July and August many open-air concerts and musical events will not start before 10pm. The choice of bars, clubs and discos is dramatically curtailed out of season, but there is always something going on.

Art Galleries

Mallorca has a buoyant art scene, and several art galleries have bars and bookshops attached – notably Fundació La Caixa and Sa Nostra in Palma. A free bi-monthly leaflet issued by Associació Independent de Galeries d'Art de Balears gives details of what some galleries are exhibiting.

IN PALMA
Fundació Barceló
Casa del Marqués de Requer, Carrer de Sant Jaume 4. Tel: (971) 72 24 67.

Fundació La Caixa
See p38.
Fundació Sa Nostra
Carrer de Concepció 12.
Tel: (971) 72 52 10.
Pelaires
Carrer Veri 3. Tel: (917) 72 04 18.

AROUND THE ISLAND
Maior
Plaça Major 4, Pollença.
Tel: (971) 53 00 95.
Galerie les Arts
Carrer Pollèntia, 43. Aleûdia.
Tel: (971) 54 63 54.
S'Estació
Carrer d'Estació, Sineu.
Tel: (971) 52 07 50.

Bars and Pubs

All the resorts have a strip of wall-to-wall pubs and bars. In Palma, the concentration is around the seedy Plaça Gomila in Es Terreno district, popular with the US Navy. In the city centre, Carrer de Apuntadores is always lively.

Casino

Mallorca has one casino, Casino de Mallorca. This is combined with the Casino Palladium, which offers dinner and variety shows and is available as an organised excursion. Gaming includes roulette, blackjack and slot machines. A jacket and tie for men, and passport are required.

Urbanización Sol de Mallorca, at the end of the motorway to Andratx (turn off at Cala Figuera), Calvià. Tel: (971) 13 00 00. Open: daily 8pm–4am; www.casinodemallorca.com

Cinemas

Programmes and times are advertised in the local newspapers. Films are usually dubbed into Castilian Spanish. Cinemas (*cine*) seem to be the only places to go for young Mallorcans, and theatres are packed for new Hollywood releases. The following are all in Palma:

Chaplin Multicines
Carrer de Bartomeu Torres, SL.
Tel: (971) 27 04 75.
Multicines Porto Pi Centro
Av Joan Miró, 154.
Tel: (971) 40 55 00.
Nuevo Hispania
Carrer de Benito Pons 4.
Tel: (971) 27 04 75.
Salón Rialto
Carrer de Sant Feliu 5.
Tel: (971) 72 12 45.

Hotels and bars in the resorts also screen English-language videos and TV programmes.

Discos and Nightclubs

There are more than 150 discotheques and nightclubs in Mallorca, providing sounds for everyone, from teenyboppers to the young at heart. Though the wilder scene is on the neighbouring island of Ibiza, several establishments have earned a reputation for their extravagant decor and light shows.

The best alternative discos tend to come and go, or at least change their names to suggest they are moving with the times. To find the beat you need to ask around in bars and clothes shops, or chat up the beach Adonises handing out flyers. Nightclubs, catering to refined spenders and dressers, can be found in some luxury hotels.

Every bar has a theme, however odd

IN PALMA
Art Deco
Plaza del Vapor, Palma. Tel: (650) 39 19 15.
Pacha
Paseo Maritimo 42. Tel: (971) 45 59 08.
Tito's
Top-rate nightclub for all.
Plaça Gomila 3. Tel: (971) 73 00 17;
www.titosmallorca.com
Zambezi Bar Night Club
C/Industria, 3, Molino. Tel: (699) 31 38 87.

ELSEWHERE
Banana
Magaluf
BCM Discotheque
5,000 capacity, state-of-the-art light
show.
Avinguda S'Olivera, Magaluf.
Tel: (971) 13 15 46.
Oliver's Jazz Club & Restaurant
Metge Llopis, 23, Porta de Pollensa.
Tel: (971) 86 75 38.
Paladium
Palma-Andratx, Andratx.
Tel: (971) 68 85 57.
El Templo del Faraon
Avda. 16 de Julio, 38–Poligono Son
Castello.
Tel: (971) 91 86 39.

Folklore and Dinner Shows
Exhibitions of Mallorcan music and
dance are staged regularly in the
summer at La Granja and Valldemossa
(*see pp56–7 & pp84–5*), and often
coincide with coach excursions.
Floorshows, barbecues, pirate
adventures and medieval banquets can
also be booked through your hotel.
Casino de Mallorca
See pp150–51.

Pirates Adventure
Dinner and yo-ho-ho. For adults only.
Carretera La Porassa, Magaluf.
Tel: (971) 13 04 11.
Son Amar
Dinner and floorshow.
Carretera de Sóller, km10.8, Bunyola.
Tel: (971) 61 75 33;
www.sonamar.com

Hotel Entertainment
Hotels like to keep you in their clutches,
and the high-class ones put on quality
live music to help guests run up the bar
bill with a devil-may-care grin. Non-
residents are welcome to join the
parties, so if your own multilingual
bingo caller is too much, try the
monosyllabic magician next door.
Programmes are usually posted up in
foyers, with regular spots each day of
the week. Don't be surprised if
performances start later than advertised.

Musical Events
Concerts and music festivals are staged
in Mallorca throughout the year,
including a programme of musical and
popular events in the resorts between
November and April. All the following
are in Palma unless stated otherwise.
Ask at a tourist office for more details of
the dates and programme.
January: classical and light music for
Sant Sebastià *festa*.
March: international week of organ
music.
March–June: spring opera season at
Teatre Principal.
July: international folk dancing at Sóller.
July–August: international music
festival in Pollença and Chopin festival

at Valldemossa. Summer serenades in Castell de Bellver and music festivals in Deià, Artà, Sóller and Santuari de Cura (Puig de Randa).

September–October: festival of classical music in Bunyola.

October: week of organ concerts in local churches.

Theatres and Concert Halls
Auditòrium
Passeig Marítim 18, Palma.
Tel: (971) 73 47 35. Tickets sold 10am–2pm & 4–9pm.
Teatre Principal
Placa Weyler 7, Palma.
Tel: (971) 72 55 48.
Ses Voltes
Parc de la Mar, Palma.
Tel: (971) 71 42 38.

Other venues for irregular music and dance events are the Bendinat Golf Club (west of Palma), Castell de Bellver (Palma), Son Marroig, Valldemossa, Sa Calobra (all three in the northwest of the island), Casa March gardens (near Cala Rajada in the northeast), and in several churches and monasteries around the island.

The Daily Bee

World news, sports reports and local issues are all covered by the English-language *Majorca Daily Bulletin*, affectionately known as the *Daily Bee*. Now over 40 years old, the newspaper is a venerable example of the outspoken visitor-pleasing publications found in many holiday destinations. Serious reporting is always spiced with the sensational and quirky.

Mallorca's international disco scene

Packaging Paradise

Mallorca's phenomenal development as a tourist island is now the stuff of textbooks. The French even coined a derogatory verb, *baléariser*, to describe this evolution, and the Mallorcan model has been copied in coastal resorts from North Africa to the Caribbean. Today, tourism is taught as a subject in the island's state-run university, and in Palma a private Escuela de Turismo (School of Tourism) draws hundreds of students from around the world to learn the art of running hotel chains, creating Paradise and packaging up holidaymakers for profit.

Though well-heeled tourists were discovering the island in the late 19th century, it was only after World War II that visitors began coming here in great numbers. In 1931 Mallorca welcomed 43,000 tourists; by 1950 there were 127,000. This sudden influx was chronicled with alarm by the island's resident sage, Robert Graves. 'Around 1951,' he wrote, 'British, French and American travellers accepted the fantasy of Majorca as the Isle of Love, the Isle of Tranquillity, the Paradise where the sun always shines and where one can live like a fighting cock on a dollar a day, drinks included.'

Mallorca still draws an artistic crowd, though most impecunious Bohemians now prefer Ibiza. The drinks aren't so cheap either, and the well-documented days of the lager-fuelled *gamberros ingeleses* (English hooligans) and their Continental equivalents are over.

mainland. If you have never been to a bullfight, Mallorca is not the best place to experiment: for the traditional drama and spectacle, go to one of the great arenas in Seville or Madrid.

Every summer is bullfight season in Palma's Plaça de Toros. There are bullrings in Inca, Muro and Alcúdia too where fights are staged to coincide with a local celebration. In season, posters and newspaper advertisements give details of the programme and how to buy tickets. Seats in the sun (*sol*) are cheaper than those in the shade (*sombra*). Organised excursions are sometimes arranged, for example, to Alcúdia, where mock bullfights with exhibitions of dressage are staged every Thursday at 6pm in the summer.

Plaça de Toros
Avinguda Gaspar B Arquitecte 32, Palma. Tel: (971) 75 52 45.
Muro
Calle Cervantes, s/n. Tel: (971) 53 73 29.

Cycling

Spring is the main season for competitive cycling when a round-island race is staged. There is a velodrome in Palma's Palau Municipal d'Esports (*see* Sports Centres, *p161*). For leisure cycling, *see pp136–7*.
Federación Balear di Ciclismo
Carrer de Francesc Faiol i Juan 2, Palma. Tel: (971) 20 84 02.

Diving

Many scuba-diving clubs and schools on the island take advantage of the clear waters off the Mallorcan coast. Diving is held in several caves and on two wrecks.

Albatros Diving
Visit six underwater grottos.
Son Servera. Tel: (971) 58 68 07.
Federación Balear di Actividades Subacuaticas
Polideportivo Son Moix, Camino de la Vileta, 40. Palma. Tel: (971) 28 82 42.
La Morena
A 60-m long cave, with air bubble and stalactites to explore.
Playa Cala Gran, Cala d'Or.
Tel: (971) 65 70 74.
Mero Diving
Diving in caves.
Cala Rajada. Tel: (971) 56 60 40;
www.mero-diving.com
Oceans Edge Dive Centre
C/Rosa del Viento s/n Sillot, Apartado 208, Porto Cristo. Tel: (971) 81 01 99.

Fishing

Porto Cristo is a favourite spot for underwater fishing, and used for world championships. Licences are required for fishing in Mallorcan waters. For sports or underwater fishing contact: **Comandancia de Marina** (*Moll Vell 1, Palma, tel: (971) 71 13 71*). For trout and carp fishing in the mountain reservoirs at Gorg Blau and Cúber contact: **ICONA** (*Passatge de Guillermo de Torrela 1, Palma, tel: (971) 71 74 40*). For information on fishing and a list of regulations contact: **Direcció General de Pesca** (*Carrer Foners, 10. Palma. Tel: (971) 17 61 00*).

Football

Mallorca is home to two teams in the Spanish football league, Real Mallorca and Atlético Baleares. Matches normally played on Saturday or Sunday evening,

5pm onward, at **Son Moix Stadium**
(*Cami dels Reis s/n, tel: (971) 22 00 20*).

Golf

The best known clubs are at Santa
Ponça and Son Vida. Competitions
are frequently held, including the
annual Balearic Open. Golfing holidays
to Mallorca can be arranged as a
package, and golf passes, giving access
to all the island's clubs, can be bought.
All courses have 18 holes unless stated
otherwise.
For information contact: **Federación
Balear de Golf** (*Avinguda Jaume III 17.
Palma, tel: (971) 72 27 53*). Some of the
main golf courses are:

WEST OF PALMA
Golf de Poniente
Tel: (971) 13 01 48.
Golf Santa Ponça I
Tel: (971) 69 02 11.
Golf de Andratx
Tel: (971) 23 62 80.
Habitat Golf, Santa Ponsa, S.L.
Tel: (971) 69 90 64.
**Lindner Golf & Wellness Resort,
Portals Nous**
Tel: (971) 70 77 77.
Real Golf de Bendinat (9 holes)
Tel: (971) 40 52 00.
Son Muntaner Golf
Tel: (971) 78 30 30.
Son Vida Golf
Tel: (971) 79 12 10.

NORTH
Golf Pollença
Tel: (971) 53 32 16.
Golf Son Termens
Tel: (971) 61 78 62.

NORTHEAST
Canyamel Golf Club
Tel: (971) 84 13 13.
Capdepera Golf
Tel: (971) 81 85 00.
Club de Golf de Pollença (9 holes)
Tel: (971) 53 32 16.
Club Golf Son Servera Pula (9 holes)
Tel: (971) 81 70 34.

SOUTH
Club de Golf Vall d'Or
Tel: (971) 83 70 01.
Son Antem Club de Golf (**Marriot**)
Tel: (971) 71 10 49.

Horse Racing

Trotting races (*carreras*) are
popular with a dedicated section
of Mallorcan society. There are
two race tracks, near Palma and
Manacor. Race meetings: Jun–Sept,
Sun from 9pm; 4pm for the rest of
the year.
Hipódromo de Son Pardo
Carretera Palma–Sóller km3.
Tel: (971) 75 40 31.
Hipódromo de Manacor
Esplá, Carretera Manacor-Artà.
Tel: (971) 55 00 23.

Riding

There are several good riding venues.
Classes for beginners and advanced
riders are available at several centres
around the island.
Club Escuela Equitación de Mallorca
Ctra, Pala-Sóller, km12, Bunyola.
Tel: (971) 61 31 57.
Club Escuela Equitación Son Gual
Crta, Establiments-Puigpunyent, km2.
Tel: (971) 79 85 78.

have a preferred brand of quality take it with you. Not all hotels and restaurants have sufficient high chairs, so if you have your own screw-on type take it. If you need to hire a car seat for a child, double check availability when making the booking. (*See also pp156–7.*)

Climate

Most people visit Mallorca between April and September when the island is usually warm and sunny. July and August are the hottest, driest months. Rain is most likely between October and March, when it can also be quite cold.

Consulates

UK: Plaça Major 3D, Palma.
Tel: (971) 71 24 45.
USA: Avinguda Jaume III 26, Palma.
Tel: (971) 72 50 51 (Vice Consulate).

Conversion Tables

See p179.
Clothes and shoes in Mallorca follow the same sizes as the Rest of Europe.

Crime

Beware of pickpockets in markets, outside tourist sights and in crowded places. If you are harassed by what the tour reps call 'colourful characters' trying to sell carnations, tablecloths or watches, keep moving and never get any money out as it will only exacerbate the problem.

Thefts can be carried out by your fellow holidaymakers too – apartments are particularly vulnerable in this respect. Never carry large amounts of cash or valuables, and always use safe

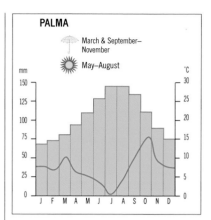

PALMA

March & September–November

May–August

mm   °C

Weather Conversion Chart
25.4mm = 1 inch
°F = 1.8 x °C + 32

deposit boxes in hotels; the small fee is worth it. Leave nothing you care about in your car or unattended on a beach. If you are unhappy about carrying your passport, get a photocopy of it verified and stamped at a police station.

Customs Regulations

Spain is part of the European Union, so there are no restrictions on the movement of duty-paid goods for personal use between Mallorca and other EU countries. The allowances for goods bought in duty-free shops (in airports or on board ships and planes), sold free of customs duty and VAT, apply to anyone visiting Spain from a country outside the European Union.

The allowances here are (per person aged over 17): 200 cigarettes or 100 cigarillos or 50 cigars or 250 gms of tobacco; 1 litre of spirits or 2 litres of table wine, and 2 litres of fortified or sparkling wine; 75 cl of perfume.

Dress

The Spanish believe beachwear and swimming costumes belong at the seaside. You may be refused entry to Palma cathedral and other churches, as well as some banks, shops and restaurants if you are considered improperly dressed. Topless sunbathing is common on many beaches, but nudism is confined to more remote beaches.

Driving

A car is not essential to enjoy Mallorca, but it is the best way to see the island at your own pace. The following are a number of tips to keep in mind:

Car Rental

Mallorca is overrun with car rental companies. If you intend to collect a car at the airport, or need a child seat, make arrangements before you

If in doubt, ask a Mallorcan policeman

leave home. Drivers normally have to be over 21 and to have held a licence for at least one year. It is advisable to take out comprehensive insurance and Collision Damage Waiver. Your travel insurance should be topped up to provide cover against your liability to a third party if involved in a motor accident. Check whether the seven per cent IVA (VAT) is included in the price.

On the Road

Drive on the right. Speed limits are 120kph on motorways, 100kph on dual carriageways, 90kph on other roads except in urban areas, where it is 50kph or as signposted. Seat belts are compulsory in front seats and back seats where fitted.

Vigilance is required at all times, particularly on mountain roads. If you meet a coach, you are obliged to reverse. Alcohol limit: 0.5gm per litre; 0.3gm per litre for new drivers with licences less than two years old.

Palma is usefully by-passed by a ring road known as Via Cintura. An *autopista* (motorway) runs west to Peguera, and another northeast almost as far as Inca. A third extends south past the airport to S'Arenal.

Parking

Parking restrictions are enforced by a scheme known as ORA. In town centres, parking lots marked in blue with Zona Blava (Blue Zone) signs can only be used with a ticket bought in advance from a nearby machine. These are valid for 30–90 minutes and have to be marked and displayed before you leave the car. Failure to do this can result in fines, wheel-clamping or towing away.

In Palma, ORA is in force within the boundaries of the old city walls: 9.30am to 1.30pm, and 5pm to 8pm, from Monday to Friday. Rules are strictly enforced. If you need to stay longer, go to a public car park.

In Palma there are car parks on the seafront and beneath Plaça Major. There are also several underground car parks. If the weather is hot, a sunshield under the windscreen is advisable. Leave no valuables behind or if you must, keep them out of sight.

Petrol

Petrol is *gasolina* and unleaded *sin plomo*. Many petrol stations are open 24 hours. Some are self-service. There are a number of petrol stations throughout the island, and all take credit cards. No change is given between 9pm and 8am.

Electricity

The supply is 220–225 volts. Sockets take round, two-pin style plugs, so an adaptor is required for most non-Continental appliances and a transformer if the appliances normally operate at 100–120 volts.

Emergency Telephone Numbers

Fire, Police, Ambulance *112*.

Health

There are no mandatory vaccination requirements for entering Mallorca, but tetanus and polio immunisation should be kept up to date. As in many

Conversion Table

FROM	TO	MULTIPLY BY
Inches	Centimetres	2.54
Feet	Metres	0.3048
Yards	Metres	0.9144
Miles	Kilometres	1.6090
Acres	Hectares	0.4047
Gallons	Litres	4.5460
Ounces	Grams	28.35
Pounds	Grams	453.6
Pounds	Kilograms	0.4536
Tons	Tonnes	1.0160

To convert back, for example from centimetres to inches, divide by the number in the third column.

Men's Suits

UK		36	38	40	42	44	46	48
Mallorca & Rest of Europe	46	48	50	52	54	56	58
USA		36	38	40	42	44	46	48

Dress Sizes

UK		8	10	12	14	16	18
France		36	38	40	42	44	46
Italy		38	40	42	44	46	48
Mallorca & Rest of Europe		34	36	38	40	42	44
USA		6	8	10	12	14	16

Men's Shirts

UK	14	14.5	15	15.5	16	16.5	17
Mallorca & Rest of Europe	36	37	38	39/40	41	42	43
USA	14	14.5	15	15.5	16	16.5	17

Men's Shoes

UK	7	7.5	8.5		9.5	10.5	11
Mallorca & Rest of Europe	41	42	43		44	45	46
USA	8	8.5	9.5	10.5	11.5	12

Women's Shoes

UK	4.5	5	5.5	6	6.5	7
Mallorca & Rest of Europe	38	38	39	39	40	41
USA	6	6.5	7	7.5	8	8.5

parts of the world, AIDS is present. Take a strong suntan cream, anti-diarrhoea pills, and, particularly if you are staying in the Badia d'Alcúdia area, mosquito repellent. If you need to consult a doctor (*médico*) or dentist (*dentista*), ask at your hotel reception. Contact the 24-hour, island-wide health centre, the Centre de Salut, which is also known as PAC.

When you arrive in your hotel or apartment check that balcony railings are secure, there is an unobstructed fire exit, cots and children's equipment are safe, and that you cannot lock yourself out by the balcony door. Report any smell of gas, check swimming pools for concealed walls before diving in, and avoid food that appears undercooked or reheated.

All EU countries have reciprocal arrangements for reclaiming the cost of medical services. UK residents should obtain the European Health Insurance Card from any UK post office. Claiming is laborious and covers only medical care, not secondary examinations (such as X-rays), emergency repatriation and so on. You are advised to take out adequate travel insurance, available through branches of Thomas Cook and most travel agents.

Insurance

Medical insurance is highly recommended – and is a pre-travel requirement with many package holidays. In the UK this can be purchased through Thomas Cook and most travel agents. Note that travel insurance does not cover liability arising from the use of a hire car, for which a top-up policy is needed (*see also* Car Rental, *p178*).

Lost Property

If you lose anything of value inform the police (*see p183*), if only for insurance purposes. The loss of a passport should be reported to your consulate (*see p177*). In theory objects that are found and handed in make their way to the local *ajuntament* (town hall). In Palma, this is at Plaça Cort 1, *tel: (971) 22 59 00*.

Media

The English-language *Majorca Daily Bulletin* provides useful local information. British and international press are widely available. Satellite TV is everywhere. Spanish TV regularly broadcasts such English classics as the Boat Race and the Grand National. The local newspapers are *Diario de Mallorca*, *Última Hora*, *Baleares* and *El Día 16*. Television channels broadcast in both Catalan and Castilian.

Money Matters

As an EU member-state, the currency in Spain is the Euro. Coins are available in denominations of €1 and €2, as well as *centimos* of the value 50, 20, 10, 2 and 1. They have a common European face but the obverse is decorated according to the designs of each member-state. The notes are €500, €200, €100, €50, €20, €10 and €5. They have no national side. Credit cards can be widely used in Palma and the resorts, but take cash as a back-up if you are going to shops or restaurants off the tourist track.